"Flame of Healing far surpasses most and effectiveness. T does not gloss over the depths to which one must delve in order to gain freedom and healing. Freda has captured the imperative essence of light and healing."

Susan Davis, Gresham, Oregon

"Flame of Healing is a study by which an individual can seek healing and hope through a Spiritual Recovery Process. It provides through Scriptures and journaling a method of working through the pain to hope and freedom from past trauma." Dr. Murl L. Silvey, Sandy, Oregon

"As I read Flame of Healing, I found myself feeling the emotions of the trauma I had gone through as a child. I followed Freda's suggestions, writing of how Christ was helping me, healing me of the hate and anger that I had bottled up. This book has brought me from the darkness of hate and anger to basking in the light of Christ."

Marilyn Wade, Gresham, Oregon

"Your book is a God Send. Because of my nursing background, people feel comfortable telling me their stories of abuse. I feel through your book, I can now know a tool to help them heal. Your book doesn't focus on the trauma. It focuses on the healing and in the process, the pain from the trauma slowly ebbs away and is replaced by a sense of faith, hope, security and even purpose." Joan, Vermont

"Your book was a tremendous help." Kathy, Oregon

"Thanks for your book — it is really wonderful. I am reading it every night before I go to sleep."

Jill, Minnesota

"I have given your book to some of the people who have come to me for pastoral counseling, before referring them to a licensed counselor... thanks for writing a book that allows others to journal and feel hope..."

Pastor Morgan K. Hjelm, Vancouver, Washington

"My friend gave me a copy... I wanted to thank you for the wonderful book. What a WONDERFUL way to learn from all this... the "work book" part... it's great !!!! Thank you so much for this book... Love your writing and knowledge !!!!!"

Julie, Sweet Home, Oregon

# Flame of Healing

# Flame of Healing

A Daily Journey of Healing from Abuse and Trauma

THIRD EDITION

Freda Emmons

CreateSpace Independent
Publishing Platform

The opinions expressed by the author are not necessarily those of CreateSpace Independent Publishing Platform.

This book is designed to provide accurate and authoritative information with regard to the subject matter covered. This information is given with the understanding that neither the author nor CreateSpace Independent Publishing Platform, is engaged in rendering legal, professional advice. Since the details of your situation are fact dependent, you should additionally seek the services of a competent professional. The author is not a physician and does not claim to be a counselor. The reader alone is responsible for the personal care of memories and emotions that may be triggered by this work.

*Published in the United States of America*

ISBN: 9781546542667

*This is for you who have been hurt . . .*
*That God would heal the wounds of your soul . . .*
*To bring you serenity – To bless you and encourage you to . . .*

"*. . . fan into flame the gift of God . . .*"
2 Timothy 1:6

## Acknowledgments

My aunts, Betty and Katherine Lamb, introduced to me the love of Christ Jesus. Their homes were a source of warmth and kindness, as well as a love that I longed for. When I stayed with Aunt Betty one summer, I attended Vacation Bible School with my cousins. There, I learned about the Lord Jesus Christ. I knew I wanted the love of Jesus that I had experienced in my aunts' homes in my own heart and life. It was then that I received the Lord Jesus into my heart. It was a turning point in my young life. I will always be thankful for my aunts' example of living in the love of Christ.

My husband, Rodney Emmons, has given me a love that is so patient and profound. He supported me through many years of healing, both encouraging and comforting me. He has given me a home of peace and three wonderful children. I am very blessed to have this man as my husband.

My friend LaVorna Tester has been faithful to the Lord in discipling me with compassion. She has been my dear sister in the Lord and has supported my efforts in writing. To have such a friend is a blessing of the Lord.

My friend Marilyn Wade has supported me through much of my healing and through the writing of this book. She has been faithful to the Lord in offering quality editing suggestions, along with prophesy about my work and my life. To have such a friend is an honor.

My friend Susan Davis has helped me to mature in Christ. She has assisted me with the editing of this book, offering insight and suggestions that both clarified as well as maintained the concept that the Lord inspired. A friend in Christ is such a blessing!

My friend Rachael Doe has brought to my life a deeper desire to seek the Lord in a new and fresh way. She prepared me to draw from the Holy Spirit and His wisdom for the writing of this work. A friend in the Lord is eternal!

My pastor is Ted Roberts of East Hill Church, in Gresham, Oregon. His diligent commitment to the Word and to the healing of broken hearts and lives through the power of God has provided profound healing in my spirit. His willingness to be vulnerable before the Lord and His people has established a vibrant ministry of healing. May God continue to bless people through this dear man!

## Table of Contents

# Introduction

This book offers slow, easy steps for healing of damaged emotions from abuse and trauma suffered during childhood, teen years, or as an adult. On each page, the gracious foundation of Scripture is the focus of one tiny step of healing. The steps in the healing process build upon each other with slow, directed movement toward healing of damaged emotions and memories.

The format of the book is based on a flame of fire. The hottest part of a fire symbolizes the core of life, God's love for you. Learning about that love and soaking it up as a sponge is the first step of healing and is pursued in Chapter 1.

The fuel of the fire exemplifies the trauma you have suffered. Christ also suffered and He died in the ultimate sacrifice of love. Chapter 2 provides a new perspective of your suffering, offering insight and grace in the power of Christ Jesus.

Chapters 3, 4, 5, and 6 explore even further the healing process. The different hues of yellow, orange, and red that are seen in afire reflect the passion of the Holy Spirit, as a flame of healing in your life. In Chapter 3, all the feelings that may have been suppressed are validated. Chapter 4 explores the process of forgiveness. Chapter 5 confirms your identity in Christ and Chapter 6 helps you to reach beyond the pain to help others.

It is possible to complete the book in one year, taking one step each day. If more time is needed for any step, it should be taken. It is okay to take as much time as is needed, for your healing — a year, two, five or ten years. Each step in the healing process is focused on Scripture. Further Bible study is encouraged; the entirety of the Bible is God's provision for healing from trauma, along with living in Christ in a fallen world. Apart from God, genuine healing is truly impossible. With God, all things are possible! I know this because in Christ, I have experienced healing as well as fullness of joy, forgiveness, and new identity in Him. May the healing touch of the Word of God bring to your heart and soul the healing and love possible in Christ.

> "I can do all things through Christ who strengthens me."
> **Philippians 4:13**

## My Journey from Pain to Healing

My youth was filled with violence and horrible pain. I lived in the turmoil of physical abuse, sexual abuse, and the emotional havoc that went with it. My brother died in a house fire before I was born; my parents' emotions were seared by the pain of their loss. At only two years old, I witnessed my sister being burned severely in an accident; she required skin grafts all over her back and was in the hospital more than a month.

I experienced physical and sexual abuse throughout my childhood and knew nothing other than the emotional pain that I lived in every day. Then I found the wondrous love of Christ and accepted Him as my Savior.

I began counseling as a young adult and the process of my healing began. Twelve years of group, individual, secular and Christian counseling, took me further on this journey to wholeness. One day I read these words from Psalm 22:10: "From my mother's womb, you have been my God." I realized that from before birth, He had been with me. I began to internalize His love for me. I realized that in everything I experienced, His Presence was with me, loving me and giving me strength to survive, to do His good will, and His perfect plan for me. The concept of this book came early, but it sat on the shelf for twelve years. My own healing needed to be more complete before I could begin to write it. Then the Lord opened the door and gave me the words.

In the process of writing, He healed a deeper, more profound trauma that I had been unable to reach. I had buried the memory that at about eleven years old, I had gotten pregnant as a result of the incest and was forced to undergo an abortion. As I am writing this book of healing, I am continuing to experience my own healing process.

This is the work of the Holy Spirit, given in mercy to me and to you. From my own healing, I have come to know that God is fully able to heal every hurt a human being may experience. That I am still in the healing process is witness to how thoroughly He works. May His grace be with you powerfully! Trust His Word; receive His Love.

# Chapter 1: Receiving God's Love

The hottest part of the flame represents the love of God. His love burns hotter than any flame ever could. The first part of healing is to receive the love that God has for you. Learn about it and allow it to soak into your soul.

1. Begin the journey of healing at the beginning with the Creator and Sustainer of all life. Just as He holds the earth in its place, so its life neither freezes nor burns up, God holds every part of your life in His hands. He keeps the intricate workings of your heart, lungs, and brain functioning to sustain the unique person you are. The place to begin healing is in awe, honoring the Creator of theuniverse, who also created you.

> "In the beginning was the Word, and the Word was with God, and the Word was God. Through Him all things were made; without Him nothing was made that has been made." **John 1:1, 3**

**Write about the God of life and how His love sustains you and gives you hope.**

2. God understands fully the pain you have experienced. He understands when the trauma happened, how old you were, how long it occurred and how much you have suffered from physical and emotional pain. He understands even those things which are so unbearably painful that you have told no one. God never grows weary of holding you in His love. His understanding and love are everlasting.

> "The Lord is the everlasting God, the creator of the ends of the earth. He will not grow tired or weary, and His understanding no one can fathom." **Isaiah 40:28b**

**Write of His immense understanding and love. Then, rest in that love.**

3. Jesus affirmed that He is God. His acknowledgment of His own eternal Presence offers hope in the midst of trauma. It is possible to put your entire life in His hands and trust Him completely with the healing of your wounded heart. Jesus is God, eternal and full of compassion and love for you, His beloved. In faith, open yourself to the process of healing by affirming in your heart that Jesus is God.

> " 'I will tell you the truth,' Jesus answered, 'before Abraham was, I am!' " **John 8:58**

**Write to the eternal Lord Jesus your longing for healing.**

4. The Father, Son, and Holy Spirit are one in love and purpose in an infinite number of ways. Yet within that oneness, each has an aspect of unique individuality. Receive in your soul blessings from the Father, from the Son, and from the Holy Spirit. Receive the love that is expressed for you by the uniqueness of the Holy Father, the glorious Savior, and the filling of the Holy Spirit.

> "For the One whom God sent speaks the words of God. For God gives the Spirit without limit. The Father loves the Son and has placed everything in His hands."
>
> **John 3:34, 35**

**Draw a simple diagram of what the love of the triune God means to you.**

5. Christ is the one who holds everything in place. He's the one to cling to when everything goes wrong. He knows the suffering you have gone through. His love will cover all the pain and heal the wounds with an eternal salve. Embrace that love; it is for you. It is from the Christ, the Creator and Sustainer of Heaven and the Earth. You are a precious child of the King, loved with an everlasting love.

> "He is the image of the invisible God, the firstborn over all creation. For by Him, all things were created. He is before all things, and in Him all things hold together."
>
> **Colossians 1:15, 16a, 17**

**Write down how you have experienced that love and how you would like to explore Jesus' love even more.**

________________________________________

________________________________________

________________________________________

________________________________________

________________________________________

________________________________________

________________________________________

________________________________________

________________________________________

________________________________________

6. You were created in the very image of God. Your beauty in Christ is reflected in your body, your personality, and your inner strength and courage. Your willingness to work through destructive experiences and seek healing demonstrates that courage. Though abuse and trauma may have left you with physical and emotional scars, your body reflects the beauty He originally intended when He created you. Thank the Lord Jesus for His creation of you.

> "So God created man in His own image, in the image of God He created him; male and female, He created them." **Genesis 1:27**

**List the physical, emotional and spiritual ways which God has placed His image in you.**

________________________________________

________________________________________

________________________________________

________________________________________

________________________________________

________________________________________

________________________________________

________________________________________

________________________________________

________________________________________

________________________________________

7. The depth of God's love is far beyond human understanding. The very best of human relationships symbolize the love God has for you. When abuse and trauma occur, the normal, healthy experience of God's love is trampled upon. God loves you with a love that is filled with glory, grace, and peace. Seek the almighty love which is there for you in Christ, even though it may seem beyond your understanding. God will bless your effort and reveal His glorious love to you.

> "As you do not know the path of the wind, or how the body is formed in the mother's womb, so you cannot understand the work of God, the maker of all things."
>
> **Ecclesiastes 11:5**

**Seek God in prayer; write down your prayer, leaving space for how God reveals His love for you.**

8. The Lord God guided your body to be formed in the way that was right for you. God alone breathed life into you. The Spirit of the Living God has been with you every moment of your life. He was with you even during the moments of abuse and trauma. He was deeply wounded by your pain and suffering. The God of love covered you, giving you strength to live on. He is with you now, as you seek healing by His grace. Lean into the Almighty One who holds you together by His love and grace.

> "The Spirit of God has made me; the breath of the Almighty gives me life." **Job 33:4**

**Write of your experience of God's Presence throughout your life.**

___

___

___

___

___

___

___

___

___

___

___

9. Ponder the holiness in which the Creator of the universe formed you. He made you to be innocent, pure, and holy, fully blessed by His love. Even though you have suffered horribly, both physically and emotionally, in Christ you are once again innocent, pure and holy, set apart for His glory. Begin to accept this innocence, purity, and holiness by faith. The healing process will confirm and strengthen the fullness of your identity in Christ.

> "For you created my inmost being; you knit me together in my mother's womb." **Psalm 139:13**

**Write of how you are stepping out in faith to accept that you are completely innocent, pure, and holy because of the grace of Christ working in you.**

10. The work of Christ in you is wonderful. He created you to be complex and beautiful as a bouquet of fragrant, exotic flowers. Rejoice in every aspect of God's creative power being released in your body and spirit.

> "I praise you because I am fearfully and wonderfully made; your works are wonderful, I know that full well."
>
> **Psalm 139:14**

**Draw a picture expressing your joy for His work in you. Use color; fill the page. The love of Christ has been created in you and now lives and reigns in you!**

11. By receiving the gift of eternal life through Christ Jesus, you have been declared righteous. This is a covering of not only your sins, but also a covering of the pain from the sins of those who hurt you. The righteousness of Jesus makes healing possible. Embrace the righteousness of Christ as if it were the warmest, most comfortable robe you've ever worn — covering you with grace, love, and hope.

> "For in the Gospel a righteousness from God is revealed, a righteousness that is by faith from first to last, just as it is written, the just shall live by faith." **Romans 1:17**

**Write how you feel, covered in the righteousness of Jesus, the Holy One.**

___

___

___

___

___

___

___

___

___

___

___

12. From the very moment of conception, there has been something deep in your soul that seeks God. Suffering abuse and trauma heightens the awareness of your need for Christ. Begin to acknowledge your complete dependence on the Almighty God. Recognize that from birth and through the time of suffering, you were utterly dependant upon Him. He is your God and loves you with a mighty love.

> "From birth I was cast upon you; from my mother's womb you have been my God." **Psalm 22:10**

**Affirm in writing how much you need God every day, every moment.**

13. The Lord God called you from before your birth. He considers you precious and has anointed you to be His child. His Spirit has drawn you to Himself and is blessing you with grace in healing. His love permeates your entire life; He wants to bring you to fulfillment in His glory.

> "Before I was born, the Lord called me; from my birth He has made mention of my name." **Isaiah 49:1b**

**Sketch how the Father God has anointed you, His child. Pray and receive His love.**

14. The Triune God knew you and loved you, even before you were born. He set you apart, from all your pain, from all your sorrow, to be holy before Him. Through this healing process, He is fulfilling His glorious purpose and is joyful in your steps toward healing. Lean into His grace and His full knowledge of your heart.

> "Before I formed you in the womb, I knew you; before you were born I set you apart." **Jeremiah 1:5a**

**Write down your thoughts and feelings of His love and knowledge of you, His child.**

15. God made everything we see out of what is not seen. His profound love fills the universe with beauty and majesty. You were uniquely created with this love. You are of inestimable value.

> "By faith we understand that the universe was formed at God's command, so that what is seen was not made out of what is visible." **Hebrews 11:3**

**Write down qualities that God has placed in you. Ponder what He has created in you, the visible beauty from the powerful Throne of Grace. Take a moment to thank God in prayer for what He has given.**

16. What a blessing and honor it is that God chose you from before the creation of the world! He chose you to be blameless and holy before Him. He made provision for living eternally in His everlasting love through Jesus Christ. By faith in Christ, you are blameless and holy. He chose you and has loved you from before the creation of the universe. You are cherished by the Holy God, Creator of the universe.

> "For He chose us in Him before the creation of the world to be holy and blameless in His sight." **Ephesians 1:4**

**Write how you feel to be chosen and loved by God.**

________________________________________________

________________________________________________

________________________________________________

________________________________________________

________________________________________________

________________________________________________

________________________________________________

________________________________________________

________________________________________________

________________________________________________

________________________________________________

________________________________________________

17. You belong to Jesus. You are His chosen, a child of the King. Think about when you were a child, before any trauma came into your life. You are as you were then, a carefree child of the living God, deeply loved. This love continued through the time of your suffering, covering you in grace and helping you to survive the trauma. Soak in the fact that you belong to Jesus; you are His cherished one.

> "And you are also among those who are called to belong to Jesus Christ." **Romans 1:6**

**Draw how you feel to be a child of the King. Praise His Name!**

18. The Holy Spirit working in you in power confirms that you have been chosen in Christ. It is more than words; your life displays the glory of His Presence in you. Your healing is a new step into that glory. As you work through the more difficult aspects of healing, be confident in the love and power given to you by the Holy Spirit.

> "For we know, brothers loved by God, that He has chosen you, because our Gospel came to you not simply with words, but also with power, with the Holy Spirit, and with deep conviction." **1 Thessalonians 1:4,5a**

**Write about the gracious work of the Holy Spirit in your life.**

19. To you who are loved by God the Father and are kept by Jesus Christ, abundance is yours. Mercy is given to ease the suffering and the trauma. Peace is given in the midst of turmoil to calm the ache of your soul. Love is given to you, that you may fully receive and reflect to those around you the love that is in Christ.

> "To those who have been called, who are loved by God the Father and kept by Jesus Christ: mercy, peace and love be yours in abundance." **Jude 1b, 2**

**Write about these three, mercy, peace, and love, and how God is blessing you in abundance.**

20. Jesus called you out of the darkness of suffering into His light. The darkness that is filled with evil and torment can no longer hold its grip. You have received His calling; you are now in His light, which is brilliant with love and healing.

> "But you are a chosen people, a royal priesthood, a holy nation, a people belonging to God, that you may declare the praises of Him who called you out of darkness into His wonderful light." **1 Peter 2:9**

**Draw a picture of yourself coming out of the darkness into the light. Be creative, to express your joy of living in the light of Christ's love.**

21. God loves you so much that He has given you power through His Spirit. The Holy Spirit is with you at every moment of this healing process, empowering you with courage, strength, hope, and love. He will be your comforter when you feel distressed. He will fulfill every deep need in grace, power, and love.

> "His divine power has given us everything we need for life and godliness through our knowledge of Him who called us by His own glory and goodness." **2 Peter 1:3**

**Write a prayer to the Spirit of the Living God and thank Him for His Presence in your life.**

___

___

___

___

___

___

___

___

___

___

___

___

22. Jesus has anointed you for a holy purpose. It will be accomplished because of His grace working in you. He has given you a spirit of willingness, openness, and seeking His will. Embrace the love the Savior has for you. Begin to live beyond the pain and sorrow you have suffered with so long. Open your heart to the glorious anointing you have from the Holy One.

"You have an anointing from the Holy One." **John 2:20a**

**Pray, asking God to reveal to you the holy purpose to which He has called you. Write your prayer, leaving space for the answer.**

___

___

___

___

___

___

___

___

___

___

___

___

23. In love, the Father draws you to Himself, through Christ Jesus' gift of redemption. Your hope is in His love now and for eternity. What has been full of sorrow can be healed because of the grace of Christ. One day, the Lord will wipe away every tear and will raise you to an eternal life of joy.

> "No one can come to me unless the Father who sent me draws him, and I will raise him up at the last day."
>
> **John 6:44**

**Write how the Father drew you to Himself — your own story of salvation in Christ. Thank Him for the hope you have in Christ.**

___________________________________________

___________________________________________

___________________________________________

___________________________________________

___________________________________________

___________________________________________

___________________________________________

___________________________________________

___________________________________________

___________________________________________

___________________________________________

___________________________________________

24. In Christ, you have eternal life. God holds you in His hand. Your destiny is eternal life with the Father, the Son, and the Holy Spirit. Because of the Holy Presence in your life, you have a hope beyond the suffering and pain of this Earth. You are covered with a love that reaches deep into your soul and heals every layer of pain. Hold onto that love.

> "I give them eternal life, and they shall never perish; no one can snatch them out of my hand." **John 10:28**

**Write about the hope and love you experience in Christ.**

25. The gift that God has given to you is unique. It will not be lessened by trauma, or by abuse. As you walk through the healing process, your gift will be fulfilled even more through the grace of Christ. You will be a blessing to God's Kingdom, by more fully loving yourself, your family and those that God brings into your life.

> "For God's gift and His call are irrevocable."
>
> **Romans 11:29**

**Write a prayer thanking God for the gift that He has placed in you. Lean into His wisdom to help you fulfill His destiny for your life.**

______________________________________________

______________________________________________

______________________________________________

______________________________________________

______________________________________________

______________________________________________

______________________________________________

______________________________________________

______________________________________________

______________________________________________

______________________________________________

______________________________________________

26. You are a gift, chosen in grace and love, given from the Father to the Son. You received the Lord Jesus as your Savior by faith. You are a part of the holy plan of creation and redemption in Christ. Christ Jesus will hold you in His loving arms and cherish you.

> "All that the Father gives to me will come to me,
> and whoever comes to me I will never drive away."
> **John 6:37**

**Take a few minutes to pray and rest in His love.
Then write how you feel in that rest.**

27. You are chosen and loved by the Almighty God. He is greater than all things and will hold you tenderly in His hand. There is nothing that can take you away from His love. The Lord will take all the hurt and transform it by grace, into blessing. You will grow closer to the Lord through this healing process. You will experience His love deeper and more powerfully because you need His grace.

> "My Father, who has given them to me, is greater than all; no one can snatch them out of my Father's hand."
>
> **John 10:29**

**Write about how it feels to receive the love of God in your soul and spirit.**

28. God loves you so much that He made provision for you to be fully reconciled with Him and live eternally. There is so much hope because the gift of life was given through Christ. One day, you will know the triune God as intimately as He knows you now. All of your pain will be removed permanently. Cling to the love God surrounds you with; lean into the hope of eternal life with a Holy God.

> "For God so loved the world that He gave His one and only Son, that whoever believes in Him shall not perish, but have eternal life." **John 3:16**

**Write about your hope and faith in Christ.**

29. God wants you to be with Him. Your faith in Christ fulfills the Father's will for you to be eternally in fellowship with Him. What joy it is to be in His will, resting in His love! The steps you are taking toward healing of deeply wounded emotions are also within the compassionate will of the Father for you. He will love you through the process, touching your heart with His Word, meeting your deepest need.

> "For my Father's will is that everyone who looks to the Son and believes in Him shall have eternal life and I will raise him up at the last day." **John 6:40**

**Write your thoughts about being in the Father's will.**

30. Jesus is the fullness of all that life is and was meant to be. He provides your every need, from the most basic physical need of food and water, to the deepest spiritual longing of your soul. Seek Him for the healing of your mind, body and spirit. Because of His grace and love for you, He will accomplish even more than what you ask. He will bless you with an abundance of joy in life. He will also bless others through you.

> "Then Jesus declared, 'I am the bread of life. He who comes to me will never go hungry, and he who believes in me will never be thirsty.'" **John 6:35**

**Write a prayer of thanksgiving to the Lord Jesus, your bread of life.**

31. The Lord is good to you. He has had compassion for you throughout your life. He gave you tremendous strength to live through the time of suffering. He is giving you now great courage to walk through the steps of healing. His compassion will hold you together in difficult days and bring you the comfort of knowing you are deeply loved. His compassion is like an exquisite, beautiful and supremely comfortable quilt that wraps you up in His love.

> "The Lord is good to all; He has compassion on all He has made." **Psalm 145:9**

**Draw a picture of how you feel resting in the compassion of the Lord God.**

32. As a child of God, you have a heart to praise Him. Try to go back to when you were a child, before suffering came to your life. Bring to your mind the innocence of your youth, when the wonderment of the world filled you with curiosity. Enfold the memory of your youthful innocence before a loving God. Give Him all your praise for your life as an innocent child and for your healing.

> "From the lips of children and infants you have ordained praise." **Psalm 8:2a**

**Draw a childlike picture of innocence and praise, for the God who created you and loves you.**

33. God has given you strength and honor. You can lean into His fullness of strength to sustain you through the healing process. He has a glorious plan for you that will bless you so much! Strength and honor and overflowing joy will be yours eternally, for you are loved by the Almighty God. It is an honor to receive such love.

> "He who formed me in the womb to be His servant — for I am honored in the eyes of the Lord and my God has been my strength." **Isaiah 49:5a,c**

**Write a prayer to the Lord and receive His love, strength, and honor.**

34. You are created in Christ Jesus. God poured His love and gracious workmanship into creating you to be the beautiful, unique person you are. In His love for you, God prepared work for you that will bless you and others. He will take all the horrible things that you experienced and in His grace will bless you with healing. He will fill you with grace and power to do the good works He prepared in advance for you.

> "For we are God's workmanship, created in Christ Jesus to do good works, which God prepared in advance for us to do." **Ephesians 2:10**

**Jot down how the Holy Spirit has blessed your life with good works already and how it may continue. Pray for wisdom for His will and guidance.**

35. In Christ, you were chosen and predestined for healing and blessing. God works out everything, including abuse and trauma, in His plan — for His ultimate glory. Through the miracle of healing, you will have a testimony of God's wonderful grace, His power over evil, and His tremendous love. In Christ, your life is for the praise of His glory.

> "In Him we were also chosen, having been predestined according to the plan of Him who works out everything with the purpose of His will, in order that we, who were the first in Christ, might be for the purpose of His glory."
>
> **Ephesians 1:11, 12**

**Write the praise that is in your heart today, for His love and grace.**

___

___

___

___

___

___

___

___

___

___

___

36. The love that God holds for you has no boundaries. In love, He adopted you to be His child and He covers you with grace. The love that expresses the limitless Trinity of the Father, the Son, and the Holy Spirit, is freely given to you. This love will restore to your heart, mind, and soul the immense value you have as a child of the Almighty God.

> "In love, He predestined us to be adopted as His sons through Jesus Christ, in accordance with His pleasure and will — to the praise of His glorious grace, which He has freely given us in the One He loves." **Ephesians 1:5, 6**

**Pray — ask God to help you receive His love. Then write down your feelings and thoughts.**

37. You are very blessed! The Holy God predestined you to be His own before the creation of time. He called you into His Presence, drawing you into the realm of the eternal. Through Jesus' wonderful gift of grace in laying down His life for yours, you are cleansed from sin and reconciled to the Father. The ultimate perfection of God's work in your life is how He glorifies you now and into eternity.

> "And those He predestined, He also called; those He called, He also justified; those He justified, He also glorified." **Romans 8:30**

**Write about being lifted up by the love of the Almighty God.**

38. The love of Christ surrounds you with His grace and power. He chose you and drew you into His love. You have a divine appointment to a place of honor in His Kingdom. He has placed before you a work of grace that will bless others and will be very fruitful. By taking steps of faith toward healing, you are beginning the journey toward tremendous fruitfulness. Begin to seek His will concerning the work of grace He has for you.

> "You did not choose me, but I chose you and appointed you to go and bear fruit — fruit that will last. Then the Father will give you whatever you ask in my Name."
>
> **John 15:16**

**Write a prayer, asking God to guide you through healing and into His divine appointment.**

___

___

___

___

___

___

___

___

___

___

39. You have received Jesus' gift of salvation and redemption. By accepting His gift of grace, you have also received the right to be His child. He has taken you out of the physical realm into the eternal. This has profound significance for the healing of abuse and trauma which you have experienced.

> "Yet to all those who received Him, to those who believed in His Name, He gave the right to become children of God — children born not of natural descent, nor of human decision or a husband's will, but born of God."
>
> **John 1:12, 13**

**You are a child of the King, born of His gracious, loving will. Write how this truth changes your life.**

___

___

___

___

___

___

___

___

___

___

___

40. One day, you will receive the fullness of your inheritance in Christ. Eternity in fellowship with the Triune God awaits you. What a wonderful hope! You are blessed by God; He has been preparing His Kingdom for you since before creation! You will experience more fully the love He has for you. He wants you to know His love now. He wants to bless you now, to bring healing to your soul and joy to your life.

> "Then the King will say to those on His right, 'Come, you who are blessed by my Father; take your inheritance, the Kingdom prepared for you since the creation of the world.'" **Matthew 25:34**

**Write about your hope in Christ and how His love helps you each day.**

41. The Holy Spirit is graciously working in your life to lead you in the perfect will of God. His Presence in your life is a confirmation of the promise that you are a child of God. The Holy Spirit will continue His work of bringing you love and healing. Open yourself even more to the quiet prompting of the Spirit.

> "Those who are led by the Spirit of God are the sons of God." **Romans 8:14**

**Write a prayer thanking Him for leading you, for being with you and loving you.**

42. Jesus' life and love for you personifies the full nature of the Triune God. At the Word of Jesus, everything came into being. His Word, the Holy Bible, is for you and will sustain you by His grace. Jesus' love is written throughout the Scriptures and is for your healing and release into joy. Immerse yourself in the Word of God by soaking each day in His grace and power. Pray, thanking the Lord Jesus for His love and His Word.

> "The Son is the radiance of God's glory and the exact representation of His being, sustaining all things by His powerful Word." **Hebrews 1:3a**

**Write how the Word has helped you and what it means to you.**

43. You have experienced suffering, which is a part of the darkness that plagues this world. In Christ, you are removed from that darkness and filled with His light. This is what makes true healing possible. In Him, you will have fullness of life. He loves you and brings you into fellowship filled with His wondrous light.

> "I am the light of the world. Whoever follows me will never walk in darkness, but will have the light of life."
>
> **John 8:12b**

**Draw what it is like to live in the light of Christ.**

44. There is hope stored up for you in heaven. What a glorious truth! The love and healing you experience here is only a portion of the joy that will be yours in heaven. Cling to this hope; the Gospel brings Good News to your broken soul. There is an ultimate hope for healing, for fullness in life, for eternal life.

> "The faith and love that springs from the hope that is stored up for you in heaven and that you have already heard about in the Word of Truth, the Gospel that has come to you."
>
> **Colossians 1:5,6a**

**Write about the hope Christ has given you and the things you hope and wait for. Trust Christ completely for these things.**

_______________________________________________

_______________________________________________

_______________________________________________

_______________________________________________

_______________________________________________

_______________________________________________

_______________________________________________

_______________________________________________

_______________________________________________

_______________________________________________

_______________________________________________

45. God's love for you is fervent. Jesus gave His life for you to be justified through Him and reconciled with the holiness of God. Because Jesus is alive by the power of God, He also gives you resurrection hope. God's love, intense and powerful, envelopes your life. This love will enable you to press on toward healing.

> "But God demonstrates His own love for us in this: While we were still sinners, Christ died for us." **Romans 5:8**

**Write a prayer of thanksgiving for God's great love for you.**

________________________________________________

________________________________________________

________________________________________________

________________________________________________

________________________________________________

________________________________________________

________________________________________________

________________________________________________

________________________________________________

________________________________________________

________________________________________________

________________________________________________

________________________________________________

46. By receiving Jesus through faith, you have been reconciled with God. The foundation of your healing is His vast love for you, and the peace that you have with Him. Christ will build on this foundation of love and peace throughout the healing process. It is important for you to allow yourself to feel the absolute peace between you and God and His abundant love for you.

> "Therefore, since we have been justified through faith, we have peace with God through our Lord Jesus Christ."
>
> **Romans 5:1**

**Write down how you feel in this perfect peace and love.**

____________________

____________________

____________________

____________________

____________________

____________________

____________________

____________________

____________________

____________________

____________________

____________________

47. The Lord has such compassion for you! It is new every morning. Hold onto His great compassion; rest in His love. Each day will bring renewed healing because of His compassion. This will give you hope for the days to come. Every day, begin with the newness of God's love and compassion for you. If difficult issues or memories threaten your emotions, come back to the pages of this chapter and soak in the awesome compassion and love of the Almighty God.

> "Because of the Lord's great love we are not consumed, for His compassions never fail. They are new every morning; great is your faithfulness." **Lamentations 3:22, 23**

**Write about God's compassion in your life.**

48. Even in the horror of abuse and trauma, God is able to bless you in His love. He will mend the situation in your life that has brought you so much hurt. By His love and grace, God will change it to be the miraculous testimony of His love in your life. Trust in the power of His love. He called you for His purpose and will bring about His good work in your life.

> "And we know that in all things God works for the good of those who love Him, who have been called according to His purpose." **Romans 8:28**

**Write about trusting God to take even this area of your life and work in it to bring about the miracle of healing.**

49. Living in a fallen world results in suffering; you have suffered greatly. Through Christ, God made provision for healing and restoration. He has called you to His eternal glory in Christ. He will bring you healing and wonderful restoration. He will make you strong, firm, and steadfast. Hold on to His promise of restoration. The love of God will cover you and comfort you as you strive for healing.

> "And the God of all grace, who called you to His eternal glory in Christ, after you have suffered a little while, will Himself restore you and make you strong, firm, and steadfast." **1 Peter 5:10**

**Write about your desire for restoration and your dependence upon God for healing.**

50. God has given you the gift of life. His love, compassion, and kindness uphold you. The Lord's utmost providence in your life is that He has watched over your spirit. He was with you throughout your ordeal. His love sustained your life and your wounded spirit. He drew you to Himself and is drawing you deeper into a relationship with Him. Receive His providence and love.

> "You gave me life and showed me kindness, and in your providence watched over my spirit." **Job 10:12**

**Write a prayer of thankfulness that the Almighty God watches over your spirit.**

51. God is love. When you place your life in His, you are filled with a love so complete, powerful, and awesome that healing is the natural result. Walk each day in the wonderful Presence and love of God. Be filled to overflowing with His love for you. Allow Him to replace each area of woundedness with grace and love. His Spirit lives in you and will continue to fill you, replacing the pain with divine love and grace.

> "God is love. Whoever lives in love lives in God, and God in him." **1 John 4:16b**

**Write how it feels to live in the awesome love of God.**

52. The Spirit of the Living God is within you, filling you with the grace of His love each day. Because of His wonderful Presence in your life, you have the power to overcome all the evil and hurtful things that have happened to you. It is not your power or strength, but rather the limitless strength and power of the Holy Spirit within you. It is the outpouring of God's grace and love to you daily. Embrace that power to overcome, by the grace of the Holy Spirit residing in you.

> "You, dear children, are from God and have overcome them, because the One who is in you is greater than the one who is in the world." **1 John 4:4**

**Write how this truth transforms your life.**

___

___

___

___

___

___

___

___

___

___

___

53. The process of healing will also strengthen and deepen your faith in God. You are stepping out in faith, trusting with your whole life that God is able to do what He has promised in His Word. With each passing day, as you receive His Word and His deep love for you, the issues that have plagued your life with brokenness will release their grip. By holding onto the love and power of the Almighty God, you will experience the restoration and blessing that you have longed for.

> "Yet he did not waiver through unbelief regarding the promise of God, but was strengthened in his faith and gave glory to God, being fully persuaded that God had power to do what He had promised." **Romans 4:20, 21**

**Write a prayer putting your trust in God's power to do what He has promised.**

______________________________

______________________________

______________________________

______________________________

______________________________

______________________________

______________________________

______________________________

______________________________

______________________________

54. Hope in the Holy God is a secure place. He has poured out His love for you through the ministry of the Holy Spirit. The foundation of healing is the love of the Almighty God and the hope He imparts to you because of that love. If you need more time to rest in His love and receive it into your soul, take it. Be secure in the love of God before taking the next step in the journey of healing.

> "And hope does not disappoint us, because God has poured out His love into our hearts by the Holy Spirit, whom He has given us." **Romans 5:5**

**Trust the Holy Spirit working within you, preparing your heart and mind for the healing made possible by His love. Write a prayer of hope.**

55. You are a child of the King, for He cherishes you. Allow the love of a gracious Father to be lavished on you, releasing you from torment to joy beyond expression. Be that child in His Presence, soaking in His love and attention. Open your heart, in childlike trust, to the awesome love of the Father.

> "How great is the love the Father has lavished on us, that we should be called the children of God!" **1 John 3:1a**

**Draw a picture of yourself with the Father, in His Presence, receiving His love. Be filled with His love.**

56. Because Christ is your Savior, you have an eternal connection with the God of the universe. His love is with you and in you. He gives you understanding about His character, about Jesus, about the Holy Spirit and about yourself. Welcome the knowledge the Lord gives you and use it to expand your perceptions and feelings. Healing and understanding will be merged by the grace and love of God in your life.

> "We know also that the Son of God has come and has given us understanding, so that we may know Him who is true. And we are in Him who is true — even in His Son Jesus Christ. He is the true God and eternal life."
>
> **1 John 5:20**

**Write about new understanding that God has given you.**

______________________________________________

______________________________________________

______________________________________________

______________________________________________

______________________________________________

______________________________________________

______________________________________________

______________________________________________

______________________________________________

______________________________________________

57. All of creation springs forth from the love of God. He created the opportunity to choose good or evil, making provision for a fallen humanity. Through Christ, there is grace and reconciliation with the Holy God. To receive God's love and grasp the healing He has for you is to honor Him. Give Him the glory for all that He has done in your life.

> "For from Him and through Him and to Him are all things. To Him be the glory forever! Amen." **Romans 11:36**

**Write down the praise and glory and honor that is in your heart for your Lord.**

58. Put your whole life into the hands of the Father who loves you. The Son gave His life for you, sending His Holy Spirit to live within you. Trust God with all that is in you. Walk in His truth. Receive His love and grace into your mind, body and spirit. Lean into His strength and power for healing. He is God in Heaven and on Earth.

> "Acknowledge and take to heart this day that the Lord is God in Heaven and on the Earth below."
>
> **Deuteronomy 4:39a**

**Write of your total dependence on the Almighty God.**

59. It is vital that you understand that there is absolutely nothing that can separate you from the love of God. As you prepare to deal with the different aspects of suffering, hold in your heart this love that permeates even evil. The love of God will get you through every day and will be the source of blessing and joy. As you are filled with His love and experience healing, you will reflect God's love to others who need Him.

> "For I am convinced that neither death nor life, neither angels nor demons, neither the present nor the future, nor any powers, neither height nor depth, nor anything else in all creation, will be able to separate us from the love of God that is in Christ Jesus our Lord." **Romans 8:38**

**Write about the love of the Lord God in your life.**

# Chapter 2: Suffering, Through the Perspective of Christ

Suffering from abuse or trauma is so devastating. The fuel of the flame symbolizes the suffering and even death that Christ endured because of His profound love for you. Isaiah prophesied that "by His wounds, we are healed." Isaiah 53:5c. In this chapter, lean into the wisdom of Scripture to understand suffering and receive the healing Christ has for you.

60. The suffering you experienced was from Satan. His is the work of lies, abuse and death. When you were traumatized, there was a loss of innocence and trust. Christ Jesus came to heal the wound of your soul. Begin this most difficult step in the healing process by placing the responsibility for that happened squarely where it belongs, on Satan. Release yourself from any guilt. Christ is fully able to restore your innocence and trust. Place your life in His.

> "He who does what is sinful is of the devil, because the devil has been sinning from the beginning. The reason the Son of God appeared was to destroy the devil's work." **1 John 3:8**

**Pray for His help in healing. Write down your prayer - and later, how your prayer for healing was answered.**

___

___

___

___

___

___

___

___

___

___

61. If you were hurt at the hands of another, it was because of their choice to sin. Without God, all there is sin and hurt. The consequences of sin are acute. Memories of physical and emotional pain sear your soul. Christ has brought His peace and mercy to your wounded spirit. Because your mind is fixed on the love of Christ, you are open to the gentle leading of the Holy Spirit. By the power of Christ Jesus, you have broken Satan's hold on you. In grace and mercy, the Spirit of the Living God will be your comforter.

> "Those who live according to the sinful nature have their minds set on what that nature desires; but those who live in accordance with the Spirit have set their mind on what the Spirit desires." **Romans 8:5**

**Write about setting your mind on what the Spirit desires in your life.**

62. The Lord God loves you so much! He considers you the apple of His eye. He cherishes you. Anyone who even touched you to cause hurt to your spirit grieves the Spirit of the Lord. He knows everything you have experienced and grieves for your pain. The Lord desires complete healing for you, in your mind, body, and spirit. He knows every step you need and will guide you in His grace. He loves you tenderly. You are the apple of His eye!

"Whoever touches you touches the apple of His eye."
**Zechariah 2:8b**

**Write about the truth revealed in this passage.**

63. The Lord hears your desperate cry for healing. He is there to rescue you from the evil you experienced. He will lift the oppressive evil and release you to the fullness of His Good Will for your life. In the process of healing, the Lord will hear every cry of pain and will meet each need with His divine provision of healing. Allow yourself to cry out to Him.

> "You hear, O Lord, the desire of the afflicted; you encourage them, and you listen to their cry, defending the fatherless and the oppressed, in order that man, who is of the earth, may terrify no more." **Psalm 10:17, 18**

**Write a prayer of need to your God; allow yourself to cry out to Him.**

64. The Lord watches over you with His wondrous love. He sees your wounded spirit as well as the love and compassion He placed in you. The hearts of those who choose to do evil are also open to His gaze. God sees everything. His mercy will be upon you because He loves you and knows how very much you have suffered.

> "The eyes of the Lord are everywhere, keeping watch on the wicked and the good." **Proverbs 15:3**

**Write about God watching over you, loving you in His grace and peace.**

65. The Lord God abhors the horrible evil that happened to you. He is grieved for the pain it has caused you. Christ Jesus gave His life that a fallen humanity may be reconciled to the Holy God and be released from the grip of the evil one. The compassion of Christ will remove from your soul the pain of victimization. Open yourself to the joy of living fully in Christ.

> "You are not a God who takes pleasure in evil; with you the wicked cannot dwell." **Psalm 5:4**

**Write a prayer asking the Lord to help you open yourself to the joy He has for you.**

66. The Lord God has the ultimate victory over Satan. This was fulfilled at the cross. He will crush Satan and his evil influence over humanity. Our God is a God of peace. The grace of the Lord Jesus is with you now, pouring His love and mercy over your spirit. In Christ, you will experience a peace that is absolute. Thank God for His victory, for His mercy and love. Ask Him in prayer to heal the pain in your soul and fill you with His perfect peace.

> "The God of peace will soon crush Satan under your feet.
> The grace of our Lord Jesus will be with you."
>
> **Romans 16:20**

**Write down your prayer and later, add notes of how God is accomplishing it.**

67. When you were stuck in the time of suffering, God's love was given to you in a very personal way, through the ministry of angels. There was a direct and immediate connection between the Father God and the angels who were with you. Through their ministry, God's love sustained you and helped you get through the time of suffering. Protection was given to your mind and spirit until you were able to process the horror that occurred to you.

> "See that you do not look down on one of these little ones. For I tell you that their angels in Heaven always see the face of my Father in Heaven." **Matthew 18:10**

**Write your perception of how angels helped you to survive; did they bring touches of God's love to your life? Then, on the following page, draw a picture of the ministering angels who brought God's grace to your life.**

______________________________________________

______________________________________________

______________________________________________

______________________________________________

______________________________________________

______________________________________________

______________________________________________

______________________________________________

______________________________________________

______________________________________________

68. God knows how very much you have been hurt. Because He loves you, He feels the trauma of your suffering. All through your life, the angel of His Presence has been with you, ministering to your spirit, with the immense love of God. The Almighty God is lifting you out of the depravity of suffering into His mercy, love, and peace. Take time to ponder His love given to you through His angels.

> "In all their distress He too was distressed, and the angel of His Presence saved them. In His love and mercy He redeemed them; He lifted them up and carried them all the days of old." **Isaiah 63:9**

**Write a prayer of thankfulness for the angel of His Presence and for God's power and love given to you through them.**

69. Just as Jesus' love for Lazarus was so profound that He broke down and wept, so is Jesus' love for you. To see His child, the one whom He created in innocence and beauty, to be so hurt, has provoked the Lord Jesus to weep — for you. He knows in His power, there will be healing for you, yet He weeps. His love for you overflows with emotion. Receive that love today and everyday. Cling to it. He is now calling you forth in resurrection power over evil, as He did with Lazarus.

"Jesus wept." **John 11:35**

**Write about living again, free from the torment of suffering.**

______________________________________________

______________________________________________

______________________________________________

______________________________________________

______________________________________________

______________________________________________

______________________________________________

______________________________________________

______________________________________________

______________________________________________

______________________________________________

______________________________________________

70. The suffering you experienced brought you down, physically and emotionally. You may feel as if you are laid low in the dust. The Lord God preserved your life in the midst of the suffering. He will continue His great preserving process in your soul, lifting you up into His perfect plan of healing.

> "I am laid low in the dust; preserve my life according to your Word." **Psalm 119:25**

**Write down how the Lord preserved you in your low place of suffering and how you feel being lifted up in grace and love.**

71. The experience of trauma, abuse, the death of a loved one, or devastating illness, is crushing to the spirit. Such traumas torment the heart and soul. The Lord God saved you and placed you under His protection, that you would be able to overcome the pain. He is close to you, comforting your broken heart.

> "The Lord is close to the brokenhearted and saves those who are crushed in spirit." **Psalm 34:18**

**Write how your spirit was crushed and how your Lord has been close to you.**

72. Jesus understands the very nature of your suffering. He, too, endured abuse, taunting and even torture until He died as the supreme sacrifice for all the sins of every human being who ever lived, even those who have yet to be born. He is well acquainted with humiliation, searing pain and emotional devastation. He also experienced divine healing, from the Father in Heaven. He is wholly able to envelop you in His grace and love, to comfort you and sustain you.

> "Consider Him who endured such opposition from sinful men, so that you will not grow weary and lose heart."
>
> **Hebrews 12:3**

**Write a prayer to Jesus; pour your heart out to Him. Lean into His grace, that you might not be weary in the process of healing.**

73. Jesus is the author and perfecter of faith. Jesus scorned the shame of the cross, yet He endured it. He scorns the shame you have endured. Place your focus on Him, for He is sitting at the right hand of the Father, in glory and honor. Jesus will help you to understand your suffering. He will perfect your faith as you put your trust in Him.

> "Let us fix our eyes on Jesus, the author and perfecter of our faith, who for the joy set before Him endured the cross, scorning its shame, and sat down at the right hand of the throne of God." **Hebrews 12:2**

**Write about how Jesus scorns the shame you endured and how fixing your eyes on Him eases that shame.**

74. Jesus knows the depth of your suffering. He is a man of sorrows, familiar with suffering. The wonderful news is that just as He lives in resurrection glory, you can live in resurrection hope. Jesus suffers with you; He is your example of divine hope. He lives in honor, love, and great glory. He imparts to you grace, healing, love, and comfort. His compassion for you knows no end!

> "He was despised and rejected by men, a man of sorrows, and familiar with suffering. Like one from whom men hide their faces He was despised, and we esteemed Him not." **Isaiah 53:3**

**Write a thank you prayer to Jesus, the One who knows your suffering and offers you hope and healing.**

75. Jesus accepted the penalty for all sin in order to bring peace to a fallen humanity. It is by His pain that you are restored and fully healed. Release all the strenuous efforts you have been striving for in your own strength. Receive by faith, your healing by His woundedness. It is a very personal healing, for Jesus loves you deeply and comprehends exactly the healing you need.

> "But He was pierced for our transgressions. He was crushed for our iniquities; the punishment that brought us peace was upon Him, and by His wounds we are healed." **Isaiah 53:5**

**Write your thoughts of releasing your efforts toward healing and leaning completely on the love and grace of Christ Jesus.**

___

___

___

___

___

___

___

___

___

___

___

76. The Holy God was with you in the midst of your suffering. He helped you to survive the trauma. Walk through the memories of your deepest pain, with the Triune God by your side. Through the Holy Spirit, you will feel the love of the Father and Christ Jesus enveloping you, meeting your every need. God will speak to you, in the quiet prompting of the Holy Spirit, about all the aspects of your suffering.

> "But those who suffer He delivers in their suffering; He speaks to them in their affliction." **Job 36:15**

**Take time just now to think through one memory and write it down. Reflect on how God speaks to you in the deepest part of your affliction.**

77. In His gracious mercy, Jesus has brought you out of the constricting misery of victimization. He has brought you to a spacious place that overflows with peace and love. He rescued you from drowning in the pain of your suffering. The Holy Lord delights in you. He is thrilled to proclaim His love to you.

"He has brought me out into a spacious place; He rescued me because He delighted in me." **Psalm 18:19**

**Write a description of the place of your pain and the place of healing Christ has brought you to. Take time to thank Him for this new place of healing.**

78. Without healing in Christ, cruelty affects every aspect of life. Trust is difficult; emotions are traumatized. Friendships are strained; sadness overflows. Christ Jesus redeems you from such cruelty. In Him, you will begin to trust again. Because of His loving grace, your emotions will become healthy expressions of your healing. Your friendships will be fulfilling relationships, for your life is based on love, in Christ. Sadness will be wrapped up in the deep love of the Savior and the refreshing joy of healing will fill your heart and soul.

> "I will save you from the hands of the wicked and redeem you from the grasp of the cruel." **Jeremiah 15:21**

**Write how Jesus is redeeming you from cruelty.**

79. The physical and emotional trauma you experienced connects you with Christ Jesus in a deep spiritual way. You carry in your body a memory of suffering so profound. The Savior suffered, in pure innocence, and died, that you would be healed. Christ identifies with your suffering; your intense understanding of suffering identifies with Him. The wonderful grace in all of this is that the love and power of the Lord Jesus Christ is revealed in you.

> "We are hard pressed on every side, but not crushed; perplexed, but not in despair; persecuted, but not abandoned; struck down, but not destroyed. We always carry around in our body the death of Jesus, so that the life of Jesus may also be revealed in our body." **2 Corinthians 4:8–10**

**Write about the spiritual bond of suffering and how you desire Christ to be revealed in your life.**

80. Belief in Jesus, the Christ, provides you with a hope in the miraculous. Jesus is the Resurrection. In Him, there is the hope of eternal life, abundant life, where there was once only a life of suffering. Allow Jesus to remove the sadness of suffering and fill you with resurrection life. One day, this will be fulfilled in the physical, with an imperishable body. Today, set yourself free to receive resurrection life emotionally and spiritually.

> "Jesus said to her, 'I am the resurrection and the life. He who believes in me will live, even though he dies.'"
>
> **John 11:25**

**Write about your resurrection hope in Christ Jesus.**

______________________________________________

______________________________________________

______________________________________________

______________________________________________

______________________________________________

______________________________________________

______________________________________________

______________________________________________

______________________________________________

______________________________________________

______________________________________________

81. Sometimes the result of abuse or trauma is a disabling physical condition. The body remembers the physical suffering you were subjected to. In the midst of such harm, God is your strength. Pursue the strength that is available in the grace and power of God. Empty yourself; embrace the strength and power flowing into you by the Spirit of God.

> "My flesh and my heart may fail, but God is the strength of my heart and my portion forever." **Psalm 73:26**

**Draw a symbolic picture of your own weakness and the strength and power of God in you.**

82. The Spirit of the Living God is living in you! The glorious work of the Holy Spirit renews your body with resurrection life. For your wounded body, this truth is profoundly healing. Allow yourself to receive this work of grace by the power of the Holy Spirit. Seek specific areas of healing of your body memories. Ask the Spirit of the Almighty to reveal to you His work of renewal and blessing within your body.

> "And if the Spirit of Him who raised Jesus from the dead is living in you, He who raised Christ from the dead will also give life to your mortal bodies through His Spirit, who lives in you." **Romans 8:11**

**Write one area of need and as the Spirit does a work of grace in that area, make a note of the healing.**

____________________________________________

____________________________________________

____________________________________________

____________________________________________

____________________________________________

____________________________________________

____________________________________________

____________________________________________

____________________________________________

____________________________________________

83. In the grace of Christ, there is a new perspective of suffering. There is never a denial of the very real pain you have suffered. There is an acknowledgment of its trauma and the opportunity in Christ for tremendous healing. The reality of eternal life breaks through the chains that once held you in bondage. The suffering you experienced, both physically and emotionally, are incomparable with the unending glory that will be revealed in you, both now and in eternity.

> "I consider that our present sufferings are not worth comparing with the glory that will be revealed in us."
>
> **Romans 8:18**

**Write about His glory being revealed in you and how it helps you release the old, worn out pain.**

84. Jesus calls you to come to Himself whenever you are weary and burdened. Healing from abuse and trauma is a process, requiring only your willingness to follow the leading of the Spirit of God. When you are overcome with the profound truth of the Word, take time to soak in its Holy purpose for your life. When you are overwhelmed by memories that are brought to the surface by the healing process, take time to soak in the profound Word, in its Holy purpose for your life. Draw near to Jesus; rest in His love.

> "Come unto me, all you who are weary and burdened, and I will give you rest." **Matthew 11:28**

**Write about how you feel when you draw near to Jesus.**

85. God's protection is different than the world's. It would be wonderful to never have any suffering. This was God's original intention for humanity. However, God also allows humankind to have free will. He allows each person to choose right or wrong, which sometimes results in horrible suffering. The Almighty God protects your spirit in the midst of that suffering. He surrounds you with deliverance through divine grace. You have been given a special area of compassion because of what you have suffered. Choose to live in the power of His grace and seek healing of your pain.

> "You are my hiding place; you will protect me from trouble and surround me with songs of deliverance."
>
> **Psalm 32:7**

**Write about the Lord's grace and power to deliver you from suffering and the compassion He has given you.**

86. Healing from abuse and trauma is really a lifelong process. What you have begun with this study of the Word of God and the routine of journaling is a lifetime of leaning upon God for help in the trouble you've experienced. He is your refuge. When the difficult days come, run to the love of God for your deepest need. He will give you strength and peace because of His great love for you.

> "God is our refuge and strength, an ever-present help in trouble." **Psalm 46:1**

**Make a note of the specific ways God is your refuge and strength when despair threatens.**

87. Your soul is the deep, hidden part of you that holds the memories of what occurred in your life. The memories amassed within your soul are physical, emotional and spiritual. From your soul, intense woundedness emanates. Cling to the Living God, to His love and compassion for the healing of your soul. Allow Him to take each and every memory and wash it in His love and grace. The memories will never fully go away, but they will be cleansed by the power of God. They will no longer torment your soul.

"My soul clings to you; your right hand upholds me."
**Psalm 63:8**

**Write a prayer asking God to cleanse the memories of your soul. Cling to His love.**

88. Hold onto the promises that God gives you in His Word. Allow them to be your comfort. A few of the promises of God are: to bring you out of misery (Exodus 3:17), to bless you (Deut. 15:6), your peace (Psalm 85:8), your salvation (Psalm 119:41), the Holy Spirit (Acts 2:39), eternal life (Titus 1:2), and the crown of life (James 1:12). Trust in the promises of God; they will preserve your life.

> "My comfort in my suffering is this: Your promise preserves my life." **Psalm 119:50**

**List the ways in which you experience the promises of God.**

89. It is reasonable to acknowledge how much you have suffered. To deny the pain and impact upon your life would be to halt the healing process. The way of healing, of abundant life, is found in the Word of God. The Triune God saturates the Word with His love. Soak in the Word; allow His Spirit to preserve your spirit with His Word of love.

> "I have suffered much; preserve my life, O Lord,
> according to your Word." **Psalm 119:107**

**Write down your favorite verse and how significant it is to your healing.**

___

___

___

___

___

___

___

___

___

___

___

___

90. Prayer is direct communication with the Almighty God. Whether your prayer is written, spoken, sung or deeply held in your soul, the Triune God welcomes your intimate communication with Him. He will give you His love and wonderful favor. Your salvation and healing has a strong foundation in the love of the Father, the grace of Jesus Christ, and the compassion and fellowship of the Holy Spirit. Take time to pray, seeking His will for whatever need you have today.

> "But I pray to you, O Lord, in the time of your favor; in your great love, O God, answer me with your sure salvation." **Psalm 69:13**

**Write how it feels to have a relationship with the Holy God, who loves you so.**

________________________________________

________________________________________

________________________________________

________________________________________

________________________________________

________________________________________

________________________________________

________________________________________

________________________________________

________________________________________

91. God is your help. He sustained you when you were hurting. He placed in your heart a desire for complete healing and the courage to strive for it. He sustains you everyday, from the very breath that you take to the deepest need of your soul. Place your trust in God alone. He knows the depth of your pain; He understands it. He will meet you there and comfort you in His divine love.

> "Surely God is my help; the Lord is the one who sustains me." **Psalm 54:4**

**Write what your need is just now and then pray for God's sustaining grace to meet your need.**

92. When you are weary of trying so very hard to overcome your pain, depend upon the Lord. He will give you strength and power. God's strength is divine in intensity and will renew your heart and soul. In His grace, The Lord will lift you out of weakness to experience a mighty power to overcome every hurt. Let this truth inspire you to live in the strength and power of the Almighty God.

> "He gives strength to the weary and increases the power of the weak." **Isaiah 40:29**

**Write briefly of your own weakness and your desire to live in the strength and power of God.**

________________________________________

________________________________________

________________________________________

________________________________________

________________________________________

________________________________________

________________________________________

________________________________________

________________________________________

________________________________________

________________________________________

________________________________________

93. Shame is the unseen emotion that incorporates all of the pain that you experienced. It is such a deep feeling that it often takes a long time to even realize it's there. Take refuge in the Lord, for He understands shame and what it does to the spirit. By faith you have received the righteousness of Christ, which covers shame in divine grace. It is His righteousness that delivers you from all the shame that was hidden deep in your soul.

> "In you, O Lord, I have taken refuge; let me never be put to shame; deliver me in your righteousness." **Psalm 31:1**

**Write down what you have been feeling in shame and release it to the righteous love of Jesus. Thank Him for understanding it and taking it from you.**

______________________________________________

______________________________________________

______________________________________________

______________________________________________

______________________________________________

______________________________________________

______________________________________________

______________________________________________

______________________________________________

______________________________________________

______________________________________________

94. The Lord God is so close to you. You have been calling out to Him for healing, for a new life of peace and love. You have come to Him in humility and truth. Your brokenness lies before Him. His compassion saturates the pain of your life to enable a divine healing. This kind of healing is not even possible in your humanity. It is only accomplished by the power of the Holy God. Trust Him to comfort you. Allow yourself to listen to the close prompting of the Holy Spirit for His love and comfort.

> "The Lord is near to all who call on Him, to all who call on Him in truth." **Psalm 145:18**

**Write two ways in which you are aware of the closeness of the Lord.**

95. The Lord God will heal the very worst pain of your life. When His work of grace is finished, the healing will be complete. The Lord's healing is often a process, in which every component of the trauma is examined, soaked in His grace, and covered in His love. A pain so deep grieves His Spirit profoundly. He desires for you His complete healing. Be willing to walk with Him through this process. He will heal you powerfully. He is the One who is worthy of praise!

> "Heal me, O Lord, and I will be healed; save me and I will be saved, for You are the One I praise." **Jeremiah 17:14**

**Write about the process of healing, putting your trust in your God. Praise His Name for the work He is doing in your life.**

96. The Lord covers you with His compassion. You are His beloved. He will give you His great comfort, that once again, you may experience innocence and safety. All of God's creation rejoices in this wonderful healing that He is giving you. You are so precious to the Spirit of the Lord God!

> "Shout for joy, O heavens; rejoice, O earth; burst into song, O mountains! For the Lord comforts His people and will have compassion on His afflicted ones." **Isaiah 49:13**

**Draw a picture of yourself, in a beautiful creation. Write a caption that shows how you feel, living in the loving compassion of the Lord.**

97. You have begun to break down evil strongholds that have held you in their grip for too long. Some of those may be guilt, depression, inadequacy, shame, evil memories, blame, unforgiveness, and anger. When your world seems to flounder, take refuge in God. He is your shield. He will accompany you through all the pain of your past and will be your deliverer. He is the sure stronghold, a place of stability and healing you can trust completely.

> "The Lord is my rock, my fortress and my deliverer; my God is my rock, in whom I take refuge. He is my shield and the horn of my salvation, my stronghold." **Psalm 18:2**

**Write about letting go of an old stronghold and trusting God to be your stronghold.**

___________________________________________

___________________________________________

___________________________________________

___________________________________________

___________________________________________

___________________________________________

___________________________________________

___________________________________________

___________________________________________

___________________________________________

___________________________________________

98. The grace of the Lord is sufficient for all your need. In working through abuse issues, or severe trauma, you may feel tremendous weakness. The grace of Christ is so wonderful; it is His power that becomes your strength in the midst of your weakness. Begin to see the pain of the past and the weakness you feel as an incentive for putting your whole trust in the power of the Living God.

> "'My grace is sufficient for you, for my power is made perfect in weakness.' Therefore, I will boast all the more gladly about my weaknesses, so that Christ's power may rest on me." **2 Corinthians 12:9b**

**Write about one area of weakness and how you can entrust this area to the grace and power of Christ.**

___________________________________________

___________________________________________

___________________________________________

___________________________________________

___________________________________________

___________________________________________

___________________________________________

___________________________________________

___________________________________________

___________________________________________

___________________________________________

99. It is very easy to fall into a pattern of looking only at the pain of the past. It is important to recognize and accept your past as a part of who you are. Healing comes when Jesus becomes the focal point on which all aspects of your life, past, present, and future, are placed. Your past can be seen through the filter of grace in Christ. When you seek the face of Jesus and His holiness, grace and love pours over your spirit. The divine strength of Christ will flow into your soul.

> "Look to the Lord and His strength; seek His face always." **Psalm 105:4**

**Write a prayer seeking the face of the Lord Jesus and His powerful will for your life.**

___________________________________________

___________________________________________

___________________________________________

___________________________________________

___________________________________________

___________________________________________

___________________________________________

___________________________________________

___________________________________________

___________________________________________

___________________________________________

100. The process of healing has steps that are sometimes very difficult and may seem to overwhelm you. One step is facing memories of what actually happened. When you allow the grace of Christ to flow throughout the experience, the memories that threatened to overwhelm you are covered in grace and love. Yes, you endured horrendous things, but you survived and have been blessed by the grace of the Lord Jesus, your Savior.

> "When you pass through the waters, I will be with you; and when you pass through the rivers, they will not sweep over you. For I am the Lord, your God, the Holy One of Israel, your Savior." **Isaiah 43:2a,3a**

**Write about the glory of His Presence, when you needed Him just to survive.**

______________________________________________

______________________________________________

______________________________________________

______________________________________________

______________________________________________

______________________________________________

______________________________________________

______________________________________________

______________________________________________

______________________________________________

101. The Lord Jesus hears every time you cry out to Him. When you seek His mercy, His compassion for you is abundant. Be confident that He receives your prayer. He offers to you His comfort by the powerful Presence of the Holy Spirit. The Holy Spirit will be with you, comforting you from this moment on, with even more intensity of His love and grace. Rest in His mercy; soak in His love.

> "The Lord has heard my cry for mercy; the Lord accepts my prayer." **Psalm 6:9**

**Write a prayer about the very worst part of your pain, seeking the Lord's mercy, love, and compassion.**

102. Be comforted in the full knowledge that God will bring an end to the violence of this world. By His Almighty power, He knows every human heart and action. In His eternal Kingdom, violence, abuse and death will be no more. In Christ's saving grace, you have been made righteous. You have a secure place, right now, in His love and mercy, and forevermore, in His Kingdom. Release the pain of your experiences to the gracious Lord.

> "O righteous God, who searches minds and hearts, bring to an end the violence of the wicked and make the righteous secure." **Psalm 7:9**

**Write about being secure in the Lord and in His righteousness.**

103. From the Lord God comes the deliverance you need. Abuse and trauma leave deep scars of awful memories and shredded emotions. The Lord's deliverance is effective. His love for you is so complete that He covers your pain by His love. The memories will fade into an acceptance of your past, with the wondrous understanding of the love of God covering you. The emotions will be healed with a divine touch. With each step you entrust to the Lord, His blessing will be on you.

> "From the Lord comes deliverance. May your blessing be on your people." **Psalm 3:8**

**Write about one thing the Lord has delivered you from.**

104. When you feel yourself sinking into sadness, sing about the Lord's love and strength. You will be lifted into His Presence. In your time of trouble, you will find refuge in the Lord. Sing in the morning to begin your day with the fellowship of Christ. Sing of His love throughout the day to keep your spirit in tune with His love. Envelop your soul in the sweetness of the Lord's love through music. Ask the Lord in prayer to help you identify the most difficult part of the day, or night, when your emotions are on edge. In that time especially, sing of the Lord's love. Soak in the worship of His glory.

> "But I will sing of your strength, in the morning I will sing of your love; for You are my fortress, my refuge in times of trouble." **Psalm 59:16**

**Write about singing of the love of God and how He is your refuge.**

105. In Christ, you are a new creation, a beautiful child of God. The old wounds have been swept away by His love. In the divine power of the Living God, the part of you that suffered is indeed gone. The new creation in you is founded on the love and power of the Lord. Release the memory of the pain and embrace the Lord's creation in you. Seek His wisdom to identify your strengths, your gifts and your abilities.

> "Therefore, if anyone is in Christ, he is a new creation; the old has gone, the new has come!" **2 Corinthians 5:17**

**Write about learning to be the person God created you to be.**

106. You are blessed because you are seeking God and His wisdom for your healing. You are taking steps toward healing with the Lord as your focus. Because you love Him, the Lord has given you a wonderful promise. You will receive the crown of life. The Holy Spirit indwells your spirit and has sealed your soul with the promise of the crown of life. When you move from this world into the eternal, the physical and emotional healing from your past will be fulfilled and the crown of life will be yours.

> "Blessed is the man who perseveres under trial, because when he has stood the test, he will receive the crown of life that God has promised to those who love Him."
>
> **James 1:12**

**Jot down your thoughts and feelings about receiving the crown of life.**

______________________________________________

______________________________________________

______________________________________________

______________________________________________

______________________________________________

______________________________________________

______________________________________________

______________________________________________

______________________________________________

______________________________________________

107. Christ was made perfect through suffering. This truth seems to be a paradox, as Jesus is Holy; He is God. The depth of His divine love needed to be expressed through suffering so that your broken, wounded spirit could come to the foot of the cross, to the One who suffered for you, and receive His love. In Christ, you are completely healed. His perfect love for you is shown through His suffering, for the healing of your woundedness. The Lord is bringing you to glory! Take time to rest in that perfect, divine love. Let it soothe any area of need you have just now.

> "In bringing many sons to glory, it was fitting that God, for whom and through whom everything exists, should make the author of their salvation perfect through suffering." **Hebrews 2:10**

**Write a prayer of rejoicing in the perfect love of Christ.**

108. When you are connected by faith to Christ Jesus, your perspective of life shifts, gradually aligning your spirit and mind to the Holiness of God. One such shift is the realization of your horrendous suffering as an extraordinary connection with Christ and His suffering. By suffering as He did, in innocence, you enter into the sufferings of Christ. The joy is that you will also enter into His glory! You will be overjoyed when His glory is revealed. It is a privilege to participate in the sufferings of Christ.

> "But rejoice that you participate in the sufferings of Christ, so that you may be overjoyed when His glory is revealed." **1 Peter 4:13**

**Write how you have this wonderful connection with Christ Jesus through suffering.**

109. Christ Jesus learned in His humanity to rely entirely upon His Father in Heaven. By placing your trust fully in the Triune God, you are following Jesus' example of obedience. With suffering, there is wrenching in your spirit. Learning to focus on God and His love for you in the midst of suffering is a huge step of healing. In the moments of pain, renew your focus on the Lord of love, the Lord of your eternal salvation. As you experience the Lord's love more profoundly each day, the pain you feel will ease.

> "Although He was a Son, He learned obedience from what He suffered, and once made perfect, He became the source of eternal salvation for all who obey Him."
>
> **Hebrews 5:8, 9**

**Focus on the deep love of the Father, on Jesus, your Lord and Savior, and on the sweet Presence of the Holy Spirit. Write down how this helps you.**

______________________________________________

______________________________________________

______________________________________________

______________________________________________

______________________________________________

______________________________________________

______________________________________________

______________________________________________

______________________________________________

110. It is very hard to understand how the most horrible experience could be good at all. Living in Christ Jesus gives you a new perspective of suffering. In Him, it is possible to understand the things you have learned through suffering. The most important lesson that comes out of suffering is a total dependence upon the love of the Heavenly Father, the saving power of Christ, and the Holy Spirit's ministry of comfort to your heart. Another lesson of suffering is empathy for others who have also suffered.

> "It was good for me to be afflicted so that I might learn your decrees." **Psalm 119:71**

**Write one or two things about God or about yourself, that you have learned through suffering.**

______________________________________________

______________________________________________

______________________________________________

______________________________________________

______________________________________________

______________________________________________

______________________________________________

______________________________________________

______________________________________________

______________________________________________

______________________________________________

111. Jesus recognized the remarkable truth of His own suffering and death; it was a gift to humanity that He freely gave, to accomplish reconciliation with God. Christ Jesus is fully able to change suffering into blessing. By grace, He will heal the hurt you've endured and bring you to a new life in Him. He will change the worst thing of your life, miraculously transforming it to be a source of deep understanding and empathy for others who suffer. You are the person you are because of the way God has taken your pain and changed it to become a blessing to you and to glorify His Name.

> "Now my heart is troubled, and what shall I say? 'Father, save me from this hour'? No, it was for this very reason I came to this hour. Father, glorify your Name!"
>
> **John 12:27,28a**

**Write about your desire for God to change your suffering into blessing.**

112. The Name of the Lord is a place to run to for safety and healing. There are many wondrous Names of the Holy God written about in the Old Testament. Some of them are Adonai, Yahweh and Sabaoth. A further study of the Names of God and His attributes will open the door to see His great love for you. Any time you have need of God's love, run to His Name and His Presence. You will find safety and compassion.

> "The Name of the Lord is a strong tower; the righteous run to it and are safe." **Proverbs 18:10**

**Write about being safe in the Lord.**

113. The worst that happened to you, things that brought you shame, terror or tremendous anger, can be healed completely through Christ. The reason to be confident in this truth is that Jesus always lives to intercede for you. As you are seeking His healing, He is ministering to you through the Holy Spirit. When the pain of very sad memories is the worst, seek Jesus even more. He will be there for you in just the way you need.

> "Therefore He is able to save completely those who come to God through Him because He always lives to intercede for them." **Hebrews 7:25**

**Write how the truth of Jesus' interceding on your behalf comforts you.**

___

___

___

___

___

___

___

___

___

___

___

114. For a moment, think about the areas of need you may have. There are physical, mental and spiritual needs that arise daily, sometimes simultaneously. Just a few needs may be finances, shelter, food, friendship, vocation, spiritual growth, fellowship in Christ, and a personal area of ministry. God will meet every one of your needs. Put your trust in Him; lean into His grace. The Lord God will take care of every need in His time, for the glory of His Name. Praise Him that He has taken care of your needs.

> "And my God will meet all your needs according to His glorious riches in Christ Jesus." **Philippians 4:19**

**List a few of your current needs and pray for the Lord's provision for them.**

115. You who revere the Name of the Lord God will receive healing. This healing is greater than what is humanly possible. A divine flow of love, peace, and joy is sent to you, as you respond to the love of God. Your will be able to, in turn, reflect this flow to others. Your healing is the beginning step of honoring the Name of the Lord in a more intense and powerful way. The relationship you have with the Father God, Jesus, and the Holy Spirit will grow in joy and peace.

> "But for you who revere my Name, the sun of righteousness will rise with healing in its wings." **Malachi 4:2a**

**Praise His Name in prayer for His healing.**
**Then write how you feel resting in His love.**

___________________________________________

___________________________________________

___________________________________________

___________________________________________

___________________________________________

___________________________________________

___________________________________________

___________________________________________

___________________________________________

___________________________________________

___________________________________________

116. You have been seeking the Lord for a long time for His healing. Your spirit has been crying out to Him since the time of your suffering. His Spirit has been with you, giving you the ability to survive and now, the ability to work through all the memories. The healing the Lord gives is lifelong and profound. It began with His love surrounding you in the midst of the trauma and continues as you receive His love. As layers of pain are released into His hand, new depths of joy and love are revealed.

> "O Lord my God, I called to you for help and you healed me." **Psalm 30:2**

**Write a prayer of thanksgiving — the Lord is mighty! You are His precious child; He is your loving Father.**

117. The foundational truths about God that are written in the Scriptures reveal His love and righteousness. As you progress through the divine process of healing, these truths become written into your life, and are reflected to others. Your life has a connection to the Holy One that is only experienced through suffering and grace.

> "I will never forget your precepts, for by them you have preserved my life." **Psalm 119:93**

**You have the wondrous precepts of the Living God written upon your soul—in His grace and love. Write how this truth makes you feel.**

118. Joseph suffered tremendously and was able to see beyond the suffering itself and the people involved, to what God wanted to accomplish through it. Take a huge step of healing by considering Satan's intention to harm you and God's higher purpose to be accomplished through your suffering. He desires close relationship with you. Your total dependence upon Him for healing each day will bring about a depth of relationship that would not have been possible otherwise. He wants to bless others powerfully through your testimony of healing in His love.

> "You intended to harm me, but God intended it for good to accomplish what is now being done, the saving of many lives." **Genesis 50:20**

**Write a thought of how good can be gained through your suffering, because of the glory of the Lord's love.**

________________________________________

________________________________________

________________________________________

________________________________________

________________________________________

________________________________________

________________________________________

________________________________________

________________________________________

________________________________________

119. As a Christian, you are a receiver of the love and grace of the Lord Jesus Christ. As you walk through the healing He is providing, you will be better able to process His love and grace in your life and reflect it to others. The suffering you lived through may not have been because of sin in your life, but for the purpose of God's love being displayed through you. As a carefully cut crystal reflects the gorgeous colors of the rainbow, so your life reflects the depth of the love and grace of the Lord.

> " 'Neither this man nor his parents sinned,' said Jesus, 'but this happened so that the work of God might be displayed in his life.' " **John 9:3**

**Write about how you want the work of God to be displayed in your life.**

120. As you transition into the next step of healing, take time to evaluate your progress. Do you need more time to work through issues of suffering with the Word of God? Healing in Christ is a lifelong process. Each day, focus on the love of God meeting your need for that day. In this way, you can experience a fullness of healing each day and a deeper constant healing as the days, weeks, and months go by. The wondrous truth of Christ's love for you is that He daily bears the burdens you feel. Lay your burdens before Him.Trust Him to provide the love and healing you need. Give Him praise, honor, and glory, that He holds you in His love.

> "Praise be to the Lord, to God our Savior, who daily bears our burdens." **Psalm 68:19**

**Write of your joy that Jesus bears your burdens.**

## Chapter 3: Identifying and Accepting Emotions

This chapter will help you to identify the feelings that have been suppressed because of the trauma that you experienced. Accepting those feelings is the beginning of healing. Receive the warmth and comfort of the Holy Spirit, as the golden hues of the fire display His passion and love for you. Emotions are a gift from God. Seek His wisdom to help you embrace them.

121. Emotions are given of God for our benefit. Just in the process of surviving severe physical and emotional pain, the emotions are often stripped bare or stuffed down until they seem to be nonexistent. The first step to healing damaged emotions is to allow healthy emotional outrage that God's law was not obeyed. It is okay to grieve with the Lord God that the law of love was broken when you were hurt. Allow the tears to come, the sadness that at the hands of others, or circumstances you could not control; you suffered so very much. As the tears flow, cover them with the love of the Lord, even going back to Chapter 1 to soak in His love.

> "Streams of tears flow from my eyes, for your law is not obeyed." **Psalm 119:136**

**Write about beginning to grieve with the Lord.**

122. The Lord loves you so much! You can approach the throne of grace with confidence that He will help you every day with every need. Suffering is often like a battering ram to the confidence that would normally grow in an individual. You may understand that you can be confident in Christ. The healing step comes in going back to a childlike trust to experience the total confidence of putting your life in the loving arms of Christ. Take a moment to imagine yourself as a child, innocent and pure, running through a beautiful, flower strewn meadow, to the glorious throne of grace.

> "Let us then approach the throne of grace with confidence, so that we may receive mercy and find grace to help us in our time of need." **Hebrews 4:16**

**Write about the feeling of confidence that you have because of His love for you.**

123. King David committed his broken spirit to the grace and compassion of God, which is written of in Psalm 31:5. When the Lord Jesus came to the end of His suffering, face to face with death, He committed His Spirit to the Father God. Both King David and Jesus trusted God with their lives. Your spirit may be so wounded that it's hard to even feel emotions. Begin with trusting God. Commit your spirit to the Lord God. Ask Him to help you feel the emotions which are linked to the trauma you suffered. You can fully trust the Lord to guard your spirit and allow the emotions to surface. He will protect your spirit from being overwhelmed and will surround you with His love.

> "Into your hands I commit my spirit; redeem me, O Lord, the God of truth." **Psalm 31:5**

**Write about committing your spirit to the Lord, the God of truth.**

________________________________________

________________________________________

________________________________________

________________________________________

________________________________________

________________________________________

________________________________________

________________________________________

________________________________________

________________________________________

124. The Lord God is aware of every detail of what happened to you. He knows the anguish of your soul. It is okay to feel that anguish. In the midst of the worst pain, God is enfolding you in His love. The healing of your emotions begins with the experience of receiving God's love as you remember the anguish that has been trapped in your soul. Rejoice in His love for you.

> "I will be glad and rejoice in your love, for you saw my affliction and knew the anguish of my soul." **Psalm 31:7**

**Write how the positive emotions of being in God's love help you with the raw emotions of your past.**

125. The beautiful innocence that God created in you was ripped away by the suffering you experienced. You were forced into a world of physical pain and emotional torment that you were unprepared for. The miracle is that you survived, by the grace and love of the Lord. As you grieve the loss of your innocence, hold onto the truth that you are a child of God. By believing in Christ as your Savior, your innocence before the Lord God is restored. This is more than being forgiven of your sin. It is a restoration of the childlike innocence of the person God created you to be.

> "I wash my hands in innocence, and go about your altar, O Lord." **Psalm 26:6**

**Write about how you feel — washed in innocence before the Lord of grace.**

126. You have walked through horrible experiences and may not have been able to quell the emotions that came upon you. As you take the step of dealing with all these emotions, the Lord God is with you. The Holy Spirit comforts you. Release any fear of evil; Satan has no power over you. God will help you with every need that arises. He will not allow you to be overwhelmed, but will comfort you.

> "Even though I walk through the valley of the shadow of death, I will fear no evil, for you are with me; your rod and your staff, they comfort me." **Psalm 23:4**

**Jot down your thoughts about this wonderful passage.**

127. Of the emotions associated with abuse and trauma, the strongest is fear. It is reasonable to desire protection and to fear physical and emotional pain. Fear can rise to huge proportions and even immobilize healthy expressions of emotions. Examine how much fear has hampered your growth as an individual. Put your trust in the Lord God. Seek Him for His wisdom about your suffering. In the power that Christ provides, set aside fear. You are always covered by the love and grace of Christ Jesus.

> "When I am afraid, I will trust in you. In God, who's Word I praise, in God I trust; I will not be afraid."
>
> **Psalm 56:3, 4**

**Write about fear in your life and setting it aside.**

128. The Lord Jesus delights in releasing you from fears that Satan throws your way. Rather than getting entangled in fear, seek the Lord and His wisdom for each day. He will deliver you from every fear, such as not being accepted, not accomplishing anything, nor experiencing normal, healthy intimacy. You are accepted, first by His love, and as you learn to accept yourself, by others. In His grace, you will accomplish great things and be a blessing to many. You will be able to experience fully, a normal, healthy and joyful intimacy.

> "I sought the Lord, and He answered me; He delivered me from all my fears." **Psalm 34:4**

**Write down one area of fear that plagues you. Seek the Lord in prayer about it and wait expectantly for His answer.**

___

___

___

___

___

___

___

___

___

___

___

129. The Holy Spirit is with you every moment. If fear grips your heart, lean on His divine comfort. The Spirit knows your struggle against fear; you can put your trust in Him. Rest in His comfort as a child lazily swings in a backyard swing. He will take the fear and remove it from you, replacing it with peace and joy—all because of His love for you.

> "And my Spirit remains among you. Do not fear."
>
> **Haggai 2:5b**

**Without any pressure to draw well, try to sketch yourself resting in the Presence of the Holy Spirit. Take a moment to ponder that the Holy Spirit is with you.**

130. The Holy One of Israel, the God of the Earth, loves you so much. The humiliation and shame that was a part of your suffering will be completely healed. Recognize the impact shame has had on your life. The Lord God is healing your spirit each day. Open the wounds of your soul and allow the Lord's grace to cleanse and purify your spirit. Receive His love for you and rejoice that the grip of shame is gone. As you live a life free from the fear of shame, its sting will be eased and forgotten.

> "Do not be afraid; you will not suffer shame. Do not fear disgrace; you will not be humiliated. You will forget the shame of your youth. The Holy One of Israel is your Redeemer; He is called the God of all the Earth."
>
> **Isaiah 54:4a,b,5b**

**Write about trusting God to heal the shame and how you feel in this new step of faith.**

________________________________________

________________________________________

________________________________________

________________________________________

________________________________________

________________________________________

________________________________________

________________________________________

________________________________________

131. The Lord God is your stronghold who fulfills your every need. He lights up the darkness where suffering has had its abode. When you were in the midst of the trauma, it was normal for you to fear those who hurt you, or the circumstances that hurt you. It was a healthy fear, a protective fear. It was part of the way the Lord helped you to survive. There is no need for fear now. Allow the Lord to heal any residual feelings of fear. Trust in His work of grace.

> "The Lord is my light and my salvation — whom shall I fear? The Lord is the stronghold of my life — of whom shall I be afraid?" **Psalm 27:1**

**Write briefly about how the Lord is healing deep wounds of fear in your life.**

___

___

___

___

___

___

___

___

___

___

___

132. God gives an innocence to each person, a trust in others for love and care. Sometimes that trust is betrayed, causing enormous pain. Healing the emotional trauma commences as you are able to see all of humanity as fallen, including those who hurt you. As you take refuge in the Lord, the Holy One who will never hurt you, a blessed healing will come. Put your trust wholly in the Triune God. Find refuge in His strength and power.

> "It is better to take refuge in the Lord than to trust in man." **Psalm 118:8**

**Write how trusting in the Lord is helping you heal emotionally.**

___________________________________

___________________________________

___________________________________

___________________________________

___________________________________

___________________________________

___________________________________

___________________________________

___________________________________

___________________________________

___________________________________

133. It is normal that you would trust in your family, friends, and in your world. When your world came crashing down around you with such devastation, trust was shattered. Put your trust in the Lord God, for He loves you and is worthy of your trust. He will be with you through the rebuilding of your life, comforting your spirit and healing your soul. Trust is a process of placing your faith in the Lord daily and seeing His love and care of you.

> "Trust in Him at all times, O people; pour out your hearts to Him, for God is our refuge." **Psalm 62:8**

**Write how it comforts you to put your trust in the Lord.**

___

___

___

___

___

___

___

___

___

___

___

___

134. As you deal each day with tiny steps of healing, it is possible that horrible memories may arise. Along with the memories, come torrents of emotions and anxiety. These often have physical responses, such as a hurt in the pit of the stomach or a lump in the throat. When these things happen, understand it is a normal response to the trauma you suffered. Seek the Lord's comfort. The love of God will cover you with divine compassion. Your body will be able to acknowledge the pain you suffered and healing will come.

> "When anxiety was great within me, your consolation brought joy to my soul." **Psalm 94:19**

**Write something of your anxiety and the Lord's comfort that eases your pain.**

135. Anger is one of those emotions that may rise up many times. God gave you the emotion of anger, so that you would be able to feel with Him the righteous anger against evil and sin. The key to dealing with anger appropriately is to entrust your anger to the Lord each day it arises. Vent to the Almighty the horror you experienced. Once you give all your anger to Him, seek His love and compassion. Allow yourself to be filled with His love, to keep you from sin.

> "In your anger, do not sin: Do not let the sun go down while you are still angry, and do not give the devil a foothold." **Ephesians 4:26, 27**

**Write about your anger and the Lord's grace to help you.**

136. The process of healing can bring sorrow, making your soul weary. It seems so hard to feel that much sorrow. It may seem a whole lot easier to shut down the emotions again, just to ease the sorrow and weariness. To do that would only prolong your pain. Instead, lean on the Lord and He will give you His strength. Allow yourself to feel the depth of your sorrow, as if walking through a long tunnel. You are not alone in this sorrow. The Lord is with you, comforting you. There is an end to the tunnel of great sorrow. It is found in the love of the Lord Jesus.

> "My soul is weary with sorrow; strengthen me according to Your Word." **Psalm 119:28**

**Write about your journey with sorrow and the Lord's comfort.**

137. When your heart is in tune with the Holy God, even sorrow takes on a new perspective. Without God, sorrow reeks of selfish misery. There is no healing, only more suffering. With the grace of the Lord Jesus Christ, sorrow is transformed into a feeling of profound sadness that is holy and selfless. It is possible to view your entire time of suffering through this godly sorrow. This will lead you into a holy forgiveness and to your own healing.

> "Godly sorrow brings repentance that leads to salvation and leaves no regret, but worldly sorrow brings death."
> **2 Corinthians 7:10**

**Write about the godly sorrow that you feel.**

138. When you choose to seek God in the midst of your sorrow, you allow Him to do a divine work in your heart and spirit. Begin to take an inward look at what Christ has already done in your life. The godly sorrow for what you suffered has produced an earnest desire for righteousness. It has also yielded an eagerness to embrace your innocence before Christ, an alarm for others who suffer as you did, and a desire to see godly justice accomplished. As you experience healing, these qualities will continue to develop through the grace of Christ.

> "See what this godly sorrow has produced in you: what earnestness, what eagerness to clear yourselves, what indignation, what alarm, what longing, what concern, what readiness to see justice done." **2 Corinthians 7:11a**

**Write a few details of what godly sorrow has produced in you.**

___

___

___

___

___

___

___

___

___

___

139. Laughter can be such a mask of very deep hurt. It is easy to let people think everything is fine. It is very difficult to set aside the laughter and the appearance of joy for the real mourning of your spirit. Take the courageous step to grieve and mourn the loss you sustained. Take the time that you need for this essential part of healing, whether a day, week, month, or a year. Only you and God know how much grief is pent up inside. Humble yourself before the Lord Jesus. Cry out to Him for His love and strength. He will lift you up and will bring you to a place of wonderful healing.

> "Grieve, mourn, and wail. Change your laughter to mourning and your joy to gloom. Humble yourselves before the Lord, and He will lift you up." **James 4:9,10**

**Write a prayer of mourning to the Lord, who loves you and knows your aching spirit.**

140. Mourning seems to be so sad, so empty; yet the Lord Jesus blesses those who mourn. The process of mourning opens your whole heart and spirit to allow a lot of emotions to be expressed. Sadness, anger, confusion and grief are just a few of the emotions wrapped up in mourning. The blessing Christ gives is His divine comfort. The Holy Spirit will be with you, as you mourn your brokenness. He will comfort you with His intimate love.

> "Blessed are those who mourn, for they will be comforted." **Matthew 5:4**

**Write about the feelings that come when you allow yourself to mourn.**

141. As you progress through grieving, the Lord will change your brokenness into a profound joy. You will no longer need to cry out to Him in despair. The burden of sadness will be lifted from your shoulders. You will feel like dancing before the Lord with childlike abandon. When this joy comes into your spirit, it is like a signal that your emotions are healing in the grace of Christ Jesus.

> "You turned my wailing into dancing; you removed my sackcloth and clothed me with joy." **Psalm 30:11**

**Write a prayer, asking the Lord for this great joy. If it has already been given to you, write a prayer of rejoicing.**

142. The Holy Spirit fulfills a miraculous work in your spirit, by confirming the truths of the Word of God to you. He overrides the evil that was done to you and testifies that you are a child of the Lord God. You are deeply loved. All of the feelings of inadequacy, abandonment and brokenness disintegrate before the holiness of His testimony to your spirit. New emotions emerge, such as confidence, joy and the ability to love others as deeply as you are loved.

> "The Spirit Himself testifies with our spirit that we are God's children." **Romans 8:16**

**List the ways in which the Holy Spirit has ministered to your spirit. Pray thankfully for His Presence in your life.**

___________________________________________

___________________________________________

___________________________________________

___________________________________________

___________________________________________

___________________________________________

___________________________________________

___________________________________________

___________________________________________

___________________________________________

___________________________________________

143. With so much healing blessing your soul, it is important to guard your heart against Satan. Often lies are hurled into your spirit; refuse their influence. The Holy Spirit will protect you. He has given you a spirit of sonship. You are a child of the King. Fear no longer has reign over your emotions. The Holy Spirit has opened the door for you to fully experience the love of God. Allow His love to reign in your spirit, with a rainbow of emotions flowing with the love.

> "For you did not receive a spirit that makes you a slave again to fear, but you received the Spirit of sonship."
>
> **Romans 8:15a**

**Write about some of the emotions you feel as a child of the King.**

144. When you accepted the Lord Jesus as your Savior, He cleansed your heart. The Holy Spirit is miraculously at work in you, healing all the areas of woundedness. You have been declared a saint, together with all those who believe in Christ Jesus. The Holy Spirit intercedes on your behalf, always in the exact will of God, to bless you. Receive the gentle prompting of the Spirit. Follow the direction of His divine guidance. Trust the work of the Holy Spirit to help the healing of your emotions.

> "And He who searches our hearts knows the mind of the Spirit, because the Spirit intercedes for the saints in accordance with God's will." **Romans 8:27**

**Write how you feel, that the Spirit of God intercedes for you.**

___

___

___

___

___

___

___

___

___

___

___

145. It is easy to fall into a pattern of just surviving. Years of holding yourself together through deep emotional trauma develop a way of living in a survival mode. There is provision for you, through the loving ministry of the Holy Spirit, to have strength and power in your inner being. Set aside the pattern of just surviving; embrace the exciting work of the Holy Spirit in your life. You will be refreshed with the strength and power He gives. It is a divine work of grace.

> "I pray that out of His glorious riches He may strengthen you with power through His Spirit in your inner being."
> **Ephesians 3:16**

**Write about setting aside old patterns of living and trusting the Holy Spirit's work in your life.**

___

___

___

___

___

___

___

___

___

___

___

146. The Lord God loves you so much! His compassion is ever present. If your prayer has been marred by the experience of trauma that you suffered, take tiny steps to seek the Lord and listen to His Spirit. Ask Him to open your heart and your spirit to His Presence. Think about one area of importance and take a few minutes to talk with the Lord. Voicing your request and thanking God for His love and compassion will help you begin a life of wonderful prayer with the Almighty Lord.

> "In the morning, O Lord, You hear my voice; in the morning I lay my requests before you and wait in expectation." **Psalm 5:3**

**Make a note of what your prayer is and how you are expectantly waiting for the Lord's answer.**

147. Often, following the Lord includes a season of waiting in your life. His purpose is fulfilled in a divine, perfect time-frame. Waiting and trusting God for His glorious answer to your prayer builds your faith and helps your healing. The Lord is worthy of your trust. Read the Word of God as you wait for His purpose and plan to be fulfilled in your life. Let the Scriptures soak into your spirit and give you hope.

> "I wait for the Lord, my soul waits, and in His Word I put my hope." **Psalm 130:5**

**Write about an area in which you are waiting for God's answer. Realize what the waiting process has done for you, and how the Word gives you hope.**

___

___

___

___

___

___

___

___

___

___

___

148. The process of healing from your experience of abuse or trauma may be longer than what you would like. It may take several weeks, or many months until the dull ache of damaged emotions eases. Be patient with yourself; take tiny steps toward healing and wait on the Lord. He knows the right time for each step. Take time for yourself, balancing family and/or job responsibilities, exercise, rest, and good nutrition with a heart that waits for the grace of the Lord Jesus. You are strong through Him.

> "Wait for the Lord; be strong and take heart and wait for the Lord." **Psalm 27:14**

**Write about waiting for the Lord's perfect timing for healing.**

149. Each morning, receive the love that God has for you. Put your trust in Him. Place everything you are — your life, emotions, hopes, and dreams — in His hands. Ask the Lord each day to guide you. Lift up your soul to Him, listening for His wisdom for your life. The Holy Spirit will guide you, in gentle, loving exhortations. Learn to live in His peace, setting aside the turmoil you have lived with so long.

> "Let the morning bring me word of Your unfailing love, for I have put my trust in you. Show me the way I should go, for to you I lift up my soul." **Psalm 143:8**

**Write how this Scripture touches your heart.**

150. Your need for healing is so deep. Suffering has affected every fiber of your being. Emotions that have been raw for years have begun to heal, but are still stinging. Perhaps your most profound prayer is for the healing of your soul and spirit. Rest in the promise of the Lord, that whatever you ask in prayer, you will receive. Believe that you have already received it and begin to live in the blessing of His love. When any of these sore emotions flare up, remember the prayer of your heart and lean into Jesus' love.

> "Therefore I tell you, whatever you ask for in prayer, believe that you have received it, and it will be yours."
>
> **Mark 11:24**

**Write about believing that you have been healed.**

151. The family of God transcends the impact of the family you were born into. If your family was a part of your suffering, God is wonderfully able to heal you and your family, if they receive Him. The family of God, the body of Christ, is more profoundly what a family was meant to be, in the love and grace of God. Receive the love and fellowship of people who live by the grace of the Lord Jesus in their lives. Begin to experience the joy of the everlasting family that is yours in Christ.

> "I kneel before the Father, from whom His whole family in Heaven and on Earth derives its name."
>
> **Ephesians 3:14b,15**

**Write about the hope that God gives you through His family.**

___________________________________________

___________________________________________

___________________________________________

___________________________________________

___________________________________________

___________________________________________

___________________________________________

___________________________________________

___________________________________________

___________________________________________

___________________________________________

152. The Lord's love and compassion has been with you throughout your life. You have been greatly in need, first with the suffering itself. In the succeeding years, the physical and emotional results of the trauma has had a devastating effect on your life. The Lord Jesus saved you and brought you into His Presence. Rest in the grace of Christ. He has been good to you and will continue to help your deepest need. Out of the worst of your pain, Christ will bring His blessing to yourself and to others.

> "The Lord protects the simplehearted; when I was in great need, He saved me. Be at rest once more, O my soul, for the Lord has been good to you." **Psalm 116:6,7**

**Write how it feels to allow your soul to rest in the love of Christ Jesus.**

153. Dozens of physical and emotional trigger points may be plaguing your spirit. Take time to identify each area of anxiety or pain. Once identified, you can release them to the process of healing in Christ Jesus. By the power of the Almighty, you are lifted up everyday to a place of joy.

> "So then, banish anxiety from your heart and cast off the troubles of your body." **Ecclesiastes 11:10a**

**Write about one area that you have released to the process of healing in the grace of Christ.**

154. It is so right to come before the Lord and ask Him to bless you. Releasing all the emotional pain of the past is a huge step. The next step is to embark on a new and exciting journey with God. Each day, fill your heart with thanksgiving for the myriad of ways God has blessed you. He is transforming the most horrible part of your life while continually healing your soul. Daily open your heart to the gracious blessings of the Lord. Ask the Lord about what is on your heart, believing in His perfect will for your life.

> "Do not be anxious about anything, but in everything, by prayer and petition, with thanksgiving, present your requests to God." **Philippians 4:6**

**Write down what is on your heart today. Then take a few moments to rest in prayer, in His Presence.**

___

___

___

___

___

___

___

___

___

___

155. The Lord is with you in a powerful way. You no longer have to live in fear or discouragement. In Christ, there is strength and courage. Reach out in new emotions, anticipation, excitement, and joy in living a life of fulfillment in Christ. Allow the peace of Christ to reign in your spirit. What was once hyper-emotional distress will be changed by the grace of the Lord to a wondrous level of emotional sensitivity. You will be blessed by the power of God working through your emotions. As you receive this gift and proclaim His grace in you, others will be blessed as well.

> "Be strong and courageous. Do not be terrified; do not be discouraged, for the Lord your God will be with you wherever you go." **Joshua 1:9b**

**Write down an area of emotion that God is changing from the negative to the positive.**

______________________________________________

______________________________________________

______________________________________________

______________________________________________

______________________________________________

______________________________________________

______________________________________________

______________________________________________

______________________________________________

______________________________________________

156. Shame once engulfed your spirit. Because of the Presence and continuing work of Jesus Christ in your life, you no longer have to feel guilt and shame. From deep within, every part of your mind, body and spirit is being released from their tenacious grip. You may find that your body is responding with renewed health. Perhaps your hair is more healthy, or your fingernails less brittle. You may have more energy. It is the work of grace in Christ. You are His and as you look to Him, you are becoming radiant.

> "Those who look to Him are radiant; their faces are never covered with shame." **Psalm 34:5**

**Describe a change in your body or spirit that has come about with healing in Christ.**

157. God has prepared the way of healing for you. He brought you to a place of safety in His grace. The wounds of your soul that were once open and festering, He is cleansing and binding in divine love. Your spirit is being renewed by the comfort and guidance of the Holy Spirit. Think of all the details of your healing in the majesty of Christ Jesus. Take a moment to sing quietly your praise and adoration to the Holy One. Be in awe of how much He loves you.

> "Praise the Lord. How good it is to sing praises to our God, how pleasant and fitting to praise Him! He heals the brokenhearted and binds up their wounds."
>
> **Psalm 147:1,3**

**Write down a few of the things you praise Him for.**

158. Satan likes to throw at you the fiery memories of your suffering. Be patient with yourself; sometimes it will still hurt with a depth you are unprepared for. Always run to God in prayer, seeking His anointing over your spirit. Satan may try to throw that familiar pain your way. Healing is a process that Christ helps you with. Emotional setbacks signal that Christ is indeed working in you and Satan doesn't want it to happen. Keep your hope and joy in Christ. Trust the Lord and His understanding rather than your own feelings.

"Be joyful in hope, patient in affliction, faithful in prayer."

**Romans 12:12**

**Write about prayer, joy and hope in your life and how these have changed your life. Or choose one of these to focus on in your journaling.**

159. The people of the early church suffered greatly for their faith. Yet they held tenaciously to hope in the Lord Jesus and the joy of the Spirit. You too have lived through great suffering and have clung to hope in Christ. Receive this great joy from the Holy Spirit. By living in the joy that is given by the Holy Spirit, your spirit is set free from the bondage of the past. This is a divine joy. It is beyond what you can lift yourself up to alone.

> "You become imitators of us and of the Lord; in spite of severe suffering, you welcomed the message with the joy given by the Holy Spirit." **1 Thessalonians 1:6**

**Write about living in the joy given to you by the Holy Spirit.**

160. When you focus on the Lord and His love, it is so much easier to release the pain of your past. Choose to live a life of joy in Christ. Keep His Word ever before you, delighting in His care for you. Seek His wisdom to help you identify the gifts that He has placed in you for His glory. Allow the Spirit to bring forth those gifts, and with the healing of your wounds, fulfill the desires of your heart.

> "Delight yourself in the Lord and He will give you the desires of your heart." **Psalm 37:4**

**Write about your delight in the Lord Jesus.**

161. You have stepped out in faith for a healing you have hoped for with all your heart and soul. You have put your trust in the Father, for His everlasting love for you. You have entrusted your entire being to the saving power of Christ. You have sought the Holy Spirit for comfort, healing, guidance, and for His constant Holy Presence in your life. Continue to deepen your faith in God; allow His power to transform all your negative experiences to work grace and beauty in your life.

> "Now faith is being sure of what we hope for and certain of what we do not see." **Hebrews 11:1**

**Write how your faith has grown since beginning your journey of healing in Christ.**

___

___

___

___

___

___

___

___

___

___

___

162. Hold onto the hope that you have in Christ. He has begun a good work in you. He will continue to heal every aspect of your pain. God is faithful. Hold onto the hope you have for a new life of peace and joy in Christ. You no longer have to be bound by bruised emotions. By receiving God's love and living in that love, you are entering into the restoration you have longed for.

> "Let us hold unswervingly to the hope we profess, for He who promised is faithful." **Hebrews 10:23**

**Write about the hope of your heart.**

163. Trauma, such as sexual abuse, the death of a loved one, or severe illness, shatters the spirit and soul. Living through such suffering, you may have felt like your soul was being tossed around a stormy sea. Hope in Christ is an anchor for your soul. Jesus' love is a secure place to rest. Take time to look deep into your soul; do you still feel that tossed around, unstable feeling? Or has the hope of Christ brought a firmness, a secure anchor to your soul?

> "We have this hope as an anchor for the soul, firm and secure." **Hebrews 6:19a**

**Write to your Lord, asking Him to be that anchor for you and to renew your hope. If you are feeling that steadfast, secure feeling, thank the Lord Jesus for His wonderful grace in your life.**

164. There may be memories and emotions that are buried somewhere deep inside. It may be really hard for you to get at them and go through the healing process of releasing them. The Holy Spirit knows what is unseen deep in your spirit. He intercedes for you, giving you divine love in your most vulnerable area of need. The Holy Spirit goes before the Throne of the Father, interceding on your behalf with such love that words cannot express the sounds that come. Receive today the joy of the Holy Spirit's gift of intercession for you.

> "In the same way, the Spirit helps us in our weakness. We do not know what we ought to pray for, but the Spirit Himself intercedes for us with groans that words cannot express." **Romans 8:26**

**Write how you feel that the Spirit of the Living God intercedes for you.**

165. A huge part of healing is coming to a place of acceptance of your past. Knowing that God loved you from before creation is a foundation of grace on which to build contentment. Now you have a new perspective of suffering. The damaging circumstances that bore deep into your soul have become a source of understanding and compassion, thus enlarging your spirit. Knowing this, that God has taken something evil and turned it to good verifies your trust in Him, which brings contentment. Receive healing and live in the love of Christ, with a contentment that truly is divine in nature.

> "For I have learned to be content whatever the circumstances." **Philippians 4:11b**

**Write about where you are in developing a deep sense of contentment in Christ.**

___

___

___

___

___

___

___

___

___

___

166. When you were stuck in pain, your mind could only focus on how much you hurt. Even though Christ saved you and you were free in Him, you were immobilized by allowing your mind to stay focused on yourself. One way Satan tries to thwart your healing is to keep from dwelling on the love and power of God. When you made the active choice to seek healing through the power of Christ, your focus shifted from yourself to the holiness of God. As you continue each day to focus on the Lord, your mind will be cooperating with the work of the Holy Spirit in you and through you. You will be fully alive, living in joy and peace.

> "The mind of sinful man is death, but the mind controlled by the Spirit is life and peace." **Romans 8:6**

**Write what it means to you to live with your mind controlled by the power of the Spirit.**

________________________________________

________________________________________

________________________________________

________________________________________

________________________________________

________________________________________

________________________________________

________________________________________

________________________________________

________________________________________

167. There may be moments that come up when your heart and mind spit condemnation at you. Satan tries to attack through thoughts of uncleanness, ugliness, unworthiness and guilt, threatening to break your spirit. Put your trust in God, who is greater than everything, who knows the truth of your heart. When you accepted Christ as your Savior, your heart was cleansed of all the filth that was sin. In Christ, you are clean and pure. You can rest in His Presence; you belong to The Truth, the Everlasting God.

> "This then is how we know that we belong to the truth, and how we set our hearts at rest in His Presence whenever our hearts condemn us. For God is greater than our hearts, and He knows everything." **1 John 3:19,20**

**Jot down the thoughts that come to condemn you and how putting your trust in God helps you to rest in His Presence.**

168. The Lord is your source of strength. When you put your hope in Him every day—even every moment throughout the day, your strength is renewed. Be open to the work of the Holy Spirit in your life. As you are healed of the tremendous burden you've carried for years, you will feel the weight of the burden being lifted from your body. Creativity, the unique gifting that God has given you, will begin to flow in your life. Use this great time of energy to learn to express God's grace and to learn the daily discipline of walking in the grace of the Lord.

> "But those who hope in the Lord will renew their strength. They will soar on wings like eagles; they will run and not grow weary, they will walk and not be faint."
>
> **Isaiah 40:31**

**Write about your renewed strength in Christ.**

169. You are righteous in Christ! Rejoice and soak in the Presence of the Heavenly Father, the Savior and the Holy Spirit in your life. If anything negative comes to you, take refuge in the Triune God. Do not allow negative stuff from an awful world to rob you of your joy in Christ. He is your refuge and strength. Trust Him for every need and desire of your heart. Praise His Name because of who He is and how much He has blessed you with the healing of your soul.

> "Let the righteous rejoice in the Lord and take refuge in Him; let all the upright in heart praise Him!"
>
> **Psalm 64:10**

**After taking a few minutes to praise Him and rest in His Presence, let your pen joyfully record your praise.**

______________________________

______________________________

______________________________

______________________________

______________________________

______________________________

______________________________

______________________________

______________________________

______________________________

170. Perhaps mornings have been difficult, with an awful awareness of the pain that gnaws at your spirit, as you awaken each day. With the healing of your spirit, there is a transforming grace in each part of the day and night. Jesus is Lord of all time. Ask Him to be with you in a profound way during whatever time of day or season the pain tends to come. He will comfort you and calm your spirit. The entire day and night will be filled with the Presence of the Holy One. Receive His joy each day.

> "Satisfy us in the morning with your unfailing love, that we may sing for joy and be glad all our days." **Psalm 90:14**

**Write about a time or season that has been difficult. Pray about whatever time or season seems to bring recurring pain to you.**

___

___

___

___

___

___

___

___

___

___

___

171. When you were in pain, worship may have seemed contrived, dull or even stunted. Your spirit was stuck, with the emotional pain and the memory of the physical pain. As you have taken these steps of healing in Christ and your emotions are being released, a joy in Christ is opening the door to experience a new worship of the Holy God. A true sense of worship, of awe and adoration for the Lord is rising up in your soul. Allow yourself to fully experience this new joy and express your joy to the Lord.

> "But may the righteous be glad and rejoice before God;
> may they be happy and joyful." **Psalm 68:3**

**Write about this transformation in your life and how it makes you feel.**

172. There are so many wonderful verses in the Scriptures that encourage you to praise God. As you are freed from the suffering that tormented your soul, reach out to the Lord in praise. Revel in the glory of His Name. Explore new ways of experiencing profound worship of the King. Taking a walk in the woods surrounds you in the beauty of His creation. Playing a musical instrument or singing a favorite hymn lifts your spirit to the glory of God.

> "Glory in His Holy Name; let the hearts of those who seek the Lord rejoice." **Psalm 105:3**

**Write about letting go of your emotions in praise of your Lord.**

173. God is your refuge every day. He gives you newness of life and peace in your soul. Be glad for His gift of grace to you. Be glad for the depth of relationship you have with Him, for the things you have learned about Him through your suffering. Be glad for God's love, which covers you eternally. Thank Him for the person He has created you to be, for the gifts and creativity He has placed in you and is now developing.

> "But let all who take refuge in You be glad; let them ever sing for joy." **Psalm 5:11a**

**List specific things you are glad and thankful for.**

174. The relationship you have here on earth with your Savior, Jesus Christ, is different from any other. You are not able to physically see Him, or touch His hands, but His Spirit is with you, so that His Presence of love and peace can be felt. Your faith is in Him. The healing of your devastating wounds is only a part of your maturing in Christ. You will continue to experience newness of life, as old baggage from the past sloughs off.

> "Though you have not seen Him, you love Him; and even though you do not see Him now, you believe in Him and are filled with an inexpressible and glorious joy, for you are receiving the goal of your faith, the salvation of your souls." **1 Peter 1:8,9**

**You are receiving the goal of your faith, the fullness of salvation. Write what this truth means to you.**

175. Through the ministry of the Holy Spirit, you have the power to know the depth of the love of Christ. This wonderful Scripture describes the love of Christ in so many dimensions. Lean into the wisdom of the Spirit to grasp more each day a love which is divine. Fill your life with that love. Let it remove all the sorrow you have experienced. Allow yourself to experience each day the love Christ has for you.

> "And I pray that you, being rooted and established in love, may have power, together with all the saints, to grasp how wide and long and high and deep is the love of Christ." **Ephesians 3:17b,18**

**Write how His love has helped you.**

176. The Lord brings to your life a peace that is so refreshing and calm! The feelings of discord that once consumed your time and energy are placed in a distant memory of what you once were. In the grace of Christ, you are now able to live every moment in a glorious new peace. It permeates your soul and spirit, relaxing muscles that were once taut with emotional pain.

> "The Lord gives strength to His people; the Lord blesses His people with peace." **Psalm 29:11**

**Write about the peace of Christ in you life, how your life is different in His grace.**

177. The Lord established peace for you. In the midst of your suffering, He allowed you a measure of peace, to sustain your soul. Perhaps it was a place you could go for safety or an emotional separation from the trauma. He helped you to find another place of peace to get you through the years until you could really begin to process the steps of healing. And now, the Lord is establishing a more profound peace for you to be able to live in His joy.

> "Lord, you establish peace for us; all that we have accomplished you have done for us." **Isaiah 26:12**

**Write how God has helped you with His peace.**

178. By the Word of God, you have been shown the path of life in Christ. Learn the Scriptures; make them a foundation for your life. The Holy Spirit fills you with joy because of His devoted Presence in your life. This joy is the beginning of your new journey in Christ. The joy of your healing, the great fellowship with the family of God and the peace in your soul are just the beginning of the eternal pleasures you will have in Christ.

> "You have made known to me the path of life; you will fill me with joy in your Presence, with eternal pleasures at your right hand." **Psalm 16:11**

**Write something about how your life has been changed by the Word, by the Presence of the Holy Spirit, or by the wonderful joy in Christ.**

179. The peace that God gives is beyond all human understanding. It is a peace that diffuses suffering with love and grace. This peace changes the abyss of pain and sorrow to be a power point in you, through which God uses to bless others. Through the loving ministry of the Holy Spirit, this peace will shield you from past pain and self-degrading thinking. Each day will bring the calming peace of God, lifting your spirit to joy in Christ Jesus.

> "And the peace of God, which transcends all understanding, will guard your hearts and your minds in Christ Jesus." **Philippians 4:7**

**Describe what this peace means to you.**

180. Your God is a God of hope. Putting your hope in Him is leaning on the arms of a wonderful Father, whose love is beyond comprehension. As you trust in Him more each day, He will fill you with such joy and peace as you have never imagined! Be open to the power of the Holy Spirit, allowing Him to flood your spirit with hope, love, joy, and peace. Release from your mind any thoughts of holding back. Allow the Spirit of the Living God to fill you with hope. Lift up your hope in Him.

> "May the God of hope fill you with all joy and peace as you trust in Him, so that you may overflow with hope by the power of the Holy Spirit." **Romans 15:13**

**Write down your thoughts of joyful hope in Him.**

181. Your spirit has suffered many torments for too long. The Lord Jesus has opened the way for the healing of your spirit. By offering yourself to the perfect will of God, you have taken so many steps of healing. The grace of the Lord Jesus will continue to be with your spirit, healing ever more thoroughly the hurts of the past. Divine grace has so much power! Draw close each day to Jesus and His sweet grace. Entrust your spirit to His.

> "The grace of the Lord Jesus Christ be with your spirit. Amen." **Philippians 4:23**

**Write about this matchless grace in your life**

___

___

___

___

___

___

___

___

___

___

___

___

## Chapter 4: Forgiveness, A Process of Grace

The passion of the Holy Spirit, reflected by the exquisite beauty of the flame, is working in your life to help you with the most difficult step of healing. Forgiveness is essential; without it you would remain in a cold world of anger, which may turn to rage. By choosing to forgive, even in the midst of the most difficult pain, you are covered by God's love.

182. The next step in the journey of healing is to begin the process of forgiveness. There are many aspects of forgiveness. The first is to realize that every person who ever lived has sinned and fallen short of the glory of God. From an earthly perspective, one sin seems different and worse than another, therefore, one person more guilty than another. From the divine perspective, all sin is abhorrent and all are guilty. Every person needs the grace of Christ.

> "For all have sinned and fall short of the glory of God, and are justified freely by His grace through the redemption that came by Christ Jesus." **Romans 3:23**

**Write about a world deeply in need of a Savior, who offers grace to all.**

183. A huge step in healing is to acknowledge before God your own sin and seek His forgiveness for any bitterness you've held onto. It is by receiving forgiveness and the release of your own heart, that you will be able to release another person in true forgiveness. Realize that it is the responsibility of each person to stand before God, either cleansed by the grace of Jesus Christ or alone before the throne to stand in His judgment.

> "Then I acknowledged my sin to you and did not cover up my iniquity. I said, 'I will confess my transgressions to the Lord'—and you forgave the guilt of my sin." **Psalm 32:5**

**Write about your feelings of learning the grace of forgiveness.**

184. If you were hurt at the hands of another, try to see that individual as someone stuck in sin. Sin is slavery to Satan. Christ demonstrated His love, for you and for all those caught in Satan's grip; He died, that *all* might live reconciled with God. Begin to see the person who hurt you as one who deeply needs Christ.

> "But God demonstrates His own love for us in this: while we were still sinners, Christ died for us." **Romans 5:8**

**Write about seeing this person differently. Pray for God's grace to cover the entire situation and give you a heart that is open to forgiveness by His grace.**

185. You have been blessed because Christ has forgiven your sins. He has the divine power of eternal forgiveness. He also teaches what forgiveness is. Even though you can remember your own sin, by faith in the shed blood of Christ, you are cleansed and considered pure. Sin no longer has its power over you. Choosing to release any person who has hurt you to the divine power of God releases you from the grip of their sin. It also releases you from a host of emotions that can become sin in your own life.

> "Blessed are they whose transgressions are forgiven, whose sins are covered." **Romans 4:7**

**Write about learning to release others into the divine power of God.**

186. Jesus has paid the price for every sin that was ever committed. It is up to each individual to accept that Jesus paid the penalty for all sin, or to ultimately stand before the judgment of the Holy God. When you seek to forgive someone who hurt you, you are not removing their responsibility for their sin. Only Christ, in His gift of salvation, is able to do that. You are, however, removing yourself from the grip of their sin. It is then between that person and God. It is like removing yourself from a waterfall of angry and hurtful actions.

> "Look, the Lamb of God, who takes away the sin of the world." **John 1:29b**

**Write about stepping out of the cascading memories of the hurt you suffered and walking into a safe place with Christ, through the miracle of the forgiving process.**

187. Think about the time before you came to Christ. Your actions sometimes were (and may occasionally still be) hurtful, to yourself and to others. Because of His great love for you, Christ made His salvation available to you. He has the same great love for those who hurt you. Ask the Lord to help you release the pain of your soul and the burden you've carried of holding those responsible in a grudge of bitterness. Seek this grace to cover you in the process of forgiveness and teach you how to forgive.

> "But because of His great love for us, God, who is rich in mercy, made us alive with Christ even when we were dead in transgressions — it is by grace you have been saved." **Ephesians 2:4**

**Write down the prayer of your heart.**

____________________________________________________________

____________________________________________________________

____________________________________________________________

____________________________________________________________

____________________________________________________________

____________________________________________________________

____________________________________________________________

____________________________________________________________

____________________________________________________________

____________________________________________________________

188. Christ has redeemed you from the ultimate consequence of sin, which is eternal separation from God. God's grace is lavished on you and on every person who accepts the gift of salvation through faith in Christ. It may be that the person who hurt you has received grace from God and the forgiveness of sins. If you are the only one holding onto the sin of that person, the only one it can continue to hurt is you. If that person has yet to come to the saving knowledge of Christ, it may be through your step into forgiveness and prayer that grace may be revealed to him or her.

> "In Him we have redemption through His blood, the forgiveness of sins, in accordance with the riches of God's grace that He lavished on us with all wisdom and understanding." **Ephesians 1:7,8**

**Write about seeking God's perfect will in the process of forgiveness.**

189. God has rescued you from the dominion of darkness. He has brought you into the Kingdom of Jesus Christ, the Lord. The dominion of bitterness and consuming anger does *not* have a hold on you any longer. In the Kingdom of true, divine love, your focus can remain on Christ, removing the constraints that bitterness once held. Rejoice that you are in His Kingdom!

> "For He has rescued us from the dominion of darkness
> and brought us into the kingdom of the Son He loves,
> in whom we have redemption, the forgiveness of sins."
> **Colossians 1:13,14**

**In whatever way is right for you, draw the difference between the dominion of darkness and the Kingdom of love in Christ.**

190. Begin to be aware that the anger, bitterness, and vengefulness within you is, in reality, sin. God is the judge of every human heart. He knows the actions of those who hurt you, as well as the desire of their heart, then and now. If you have been a victim of circumstances, such as serious illness or the death of a loved one, you may even hold anger toward God. God's love is still there for you, even in the midst of sin. Seek the forgiveness of Christ for any miserable feeling you have toward another or toward Him. Ask the Lord to cleanse it completely and fill you with love.

> "Have mercy on me, O God, according to your unfailing love; according to your great compassion blot out my transgressions." **Psalm 51:1**

**Write how you feel with the burden of your own sin gone.**

191. The Word of God will continue to lead you in the path of forgiveness and healing. Satan may try to sting you again with the memory of your suffering. Lean upon the Word. With the Word in your heart, you will be lifted above the sharp pangs of pain from the past. You will also experience more depth of forgiveness. Christ is cleansing your heart each day. Soon there is no room for anger and bitterness to reside.

> "I have hidden your Word in my heart that I might not sin against you." **Psalm 119:11**

**Write about the Word of God and how it has helped you.**

192. God looks directly at the heart. He sees beyond the hidden actions, nice words, and sweet facial expressions that come so easy to humankind. He knows your heart, that you are earnestly seeking His will for your life. Even when you slip up and allow bitterness to seep into your spirit, He knows that deep in your heart, your desire is for His love and forgiveness to pervade your heart. He also knows well those with a perverse heart, who continue to deny Him and revel in their sin. When you release your past and the people in it to God, you can rest in His perfect knowledge and judgment.

> "The Lord detests men of perverse heart but He delights in those whose ways are blameless." **Proverbs 11:20**

**Write how this truth frees you from the bondage of judging others.**

____________________

____________________

____________________

____________________

____________________

____________________

____________________

____________________

____________________

____________________

193. Sin has so many consequences. You have suffered physical and emotional trauma because of another's choice to sin. What may not be apparent is the great level of consequence that same sin held in that individual's life. The pain of being snared in sin, as an animal entrapped by a metal-toothed trap, would be frightening. As a righteous one, in the grace of Christ, you are able to rejoice because your sin has been forgiven. Ask God to help you personally release those who hurt you and also to help you pray for them to receive ultimate forgiveness in His grace.

> "An evil man is snared by his own sin, but a righteous one can sing and be glad." **Proverbs 29:6**

**Write how it helps you to commit your feelings to prayer.**

________________________________________________

________________________________________________

________________________________________________

________________________________________________

________________________________________________

________________________________________________

________________________________________________

________________________________________________

________________________________________________

________________________________________________

________________________________________________

194. Many people do not even consider the holiness of God and His wrath upon those who deny Him and destroy those He loves. His holy judgment is punishment enough for those who hurt you. You can trust in His judgment. Entrust your past and your pain to the Almighty God. Know that those who hurt you have the opportunity to seek the grace of Christ for forgiveness for their sin, or face the depravity of their sin and God's eternal judgment. Forgiveness is trusting God fully to be the judge on your behalf.

> "Don't you know that you yourselves are God's temple and that God's Spirit lives in you? If anyone destroys God's temple, God will destroy him; for God's temple is sacred, and you are that temple." **1 Corinthians 3:16,17**

**Write about trusting God in this way, with your whole life and your deep pain.**

195. Perhaps there are things that happened to you that were so horrendous that you were not able to tell anyone. They seem to be hidden in the dark recesses of the past, an awful memory that haunts you. No action is secret before God. He knows every detail of what was done to you and who did it. His judgment is secure; they will be held accountable even for the hidden sins. Ask God to help you release those who caused you deep, hidden pain, that you would no longer be subject to the effect of their sin.

> "Break the arm of the wicked and evil man; call him to account for his wickedness that would not be found out."
>
> **Psalm 10:15**

**Write how this frees you to a new life of peace.**

196. There may be some things in your past that remain hidden to your conscious mind, because they were so full of horror that you blocked them out in order to survive. God knows even those things that you may not fully be aware of, what happened, how, where and when it happened and who was involved. Do not feel shamed before the divine knowledge of God. His love and compassion for you is full of grace. Those who hurt you will have to give an account for their actions. Divine judgment, upon those who hurt those who are innocent, will indeed be full of God's wrath.

> "Nothing in all creation is hidden from God's sight. Everything is uncovered and laid bare before the eyes of Him to whom we must give account." **Hebrews 4:13**

**Describe in writing the comfort of knowing the hidden things of your past are laid bare before God.**

______________________________________________

______________________________________________

______________________________________________

______________________________________________

______________________________________________

______________________________________________

______________________________________________

______________________________________________

______________________________________________

______________________________________________

197. You are righteous in Christ and are blessed by His love. The Lord gives you assurance by His Word that those who are wicked in their hearts and in their actions will not go unpunished. His righteous anger and judgment is ample for their choice to remain wicked. You are given freedom from their wickedness. Let go of the individuals who hurt you. Release them to God, for His work of either wrath or grace, by the choice of their own hearts. Learn to live a new life of grace, a freedom from the bondage of bitterness and even hatred.

> "Be sure of this: The wicked will not go unpunished, but those who are righteous will go free." **Proverbs 11:21**

**Write about your true freedom in Christ.**

________________________________________

________________________________________

________________________________________

________________________________________

________________________________________

________________________________________

________________________________________

________________________________________

________________________________________

________________________________________

________________________________________

198. It seems too often in society, in the human system of justice, the innocent are deprived of justice. An easy response is to want to take vengeance, when the law seems to show partiality to the wicked and deny justice to the innocent. It is important to set aside earthly feelings of vengeance and put your trust in the Holy God, who will never deprive the innocent of justice. You are innocent, a victim of wicked actions. Allow the Creator of heaven and earth to be your advocate.

> "It is not good to be partial to the wicked or to deprive the innocent of justice." **Proverbs 18:5**

**Write about entrusting even your feelings of vengeance to the Almighty God.**

199. It is a mystery that God can search the heart and the mind. It is beyond human experience and even comprehension that such knowledge is possible. The holiness of God encompasses His divine knowledge. God understands every detail of the suffering you experienced, the brokenness it caused in your life and the hearts and minds of those who hurt you. Trust in His knowledge, in His deep love for you and the promise of His Word for divine judgment.

> "I the Lord search the heart and examine the mind, to reward a man according to his conduct, according to what his deeds deserve." **Jeremiah 17:10**

**Write about the divine knowledge that God has about your suffering, and how it releases you from holding onto those responsible for your pain.**

200. The Lord knows the heart of each person. He is willing to forgive every sin because of His great love. He made provision for forgiveness through Christ. It is an individual, personal choice to receive His forgiveness or to reject it. God gives a holy example of complete forgiveness through the shed blood of Jesus Christ. He wipes clean the souls of those who receive Christ. Such love is possible in your life because of the work of the Holy Spirit in your spirit.

> "Forgive, and deal with each man according to all he does, since you know his heart (for You alone know the hearts of men)." **2 Chronicles 6:30b**

**Write about learning to follow His example of love and forgiveness.**

201. The Word of God holds a mystery that is beyond comprehension. It is not like any other written work. It is living and active. As you are reaching out for God, He is opening your heart and soul to His wisdom through His Word. Keep your heart and mind open to what the Lord God is teaching you. Walking through the process of forgiveness may be the most difficult part of healing. It may be that your spirit needs to be untangled from its hold on the past and any sin that has attached itself to your heart.

> "For the Word of God is living and active. Sharper than any double-edged sword, it penetrates even to dividing soul and spirit, joints and marrow; it judges the thoughts and attitudes of the heart." **Hebrews 4:12**

**Write about the living Word in your life.**

202. It is all right to seek to understand the Lord's vengeance on those who have hurt you. God is the only true judge; His judgment is righteous and holy. Keep in mind His grace is ever ready for those who are willing to turn from their arrogance to seek His forgiveness. In His divine knowledge, God is fully able to be your advocate for justice and reign in grace and love. Keep your focus on Him, rather than continuing to look at the need for vengeance. Trust God to take care of it for you. Focus on His precepts, given in His Word. Keep your thoughts on the wonderful grace of God in your life and what He is teaching you through His Word.

> "May the arrogant be put to shame for wronging me without cause; but I will meditate on your precepts."
> **Psalm 119:78**

**Write about meditating on the things of God.**

__________________________________________

__________________________________________

__________________________________________

__________________________________________

__________________________________________

__________________________________________

__________________________________________

__________________________________________

__________________________________________

__________________________________________

203. God gives you an understanding of evil so that you can separate the evil action from the individual, who is stuck in the grip of sin. God shows by example how to have compassion for the person and hate the evil. The Lord is guarding your life and helping you to be completely delivered from the evil of your trauma. Love the Lord and His wisdom. Hate the evil and the source of evil, Satan.

> "Let those who love the Lord hate evil, for He guards the lives of His faithful ones and delivers them from the hand of the wicked." **Psalm 97:10**

**Write about leaning on God for wisdom in your life.**

204. When you were subjected to suffering, a variety of responses may have occurred. In trying to protect yourself, even after the trauma, you may have found yourself lashing out at others. This is Satan's twisting of your emotions to cause even more pain and evil. If you have experienced this, seek the Lord's grace and forgiveness. Ask Him to help you not become a part of the violence. Seek the holiness of God to be in your own life. Ask God in prayer to help you to forgive yourself for any time you were lured to take part in evil.

> "Let not my heart be drawn to what is evil, to take part in wicked deeds." **Psalm 141:4a**

**Write about forgiving yourself and the grace that is now in your heart, keeping you from evil.**

____________________________________________________________

____________________________________________________________

____________________________________________________________

____________________________________________________________

____________________________________________________________

____________________________________________________________

____________________________________________________________

____________________________________________________________

____________________________________________________________

____________________________________________________________

205. The Lord hears every prayer of your soul. He knows the depth of your pain and longing to be free from your past. Your prayer for healing is covered in the grace of the Lord Jesus. Continue your prayers for every part of this journey. You are righteous in Christ. As you seek the Lord earnestly, acknowledge with sadness the separation from God of those who remain evil in their hearts. Have compassion for those who hurt you. Do not wish for them an eternity separated from God. Compassion is the foundation of forgiveness.

> "The Lord is far from the wicked but He hears the prayer of the righteous." **Proverbs 15:29**

**Write about your close relationship with the Lord and the realization of how far away from the Lord the wicked are.**

206. In a season of learning about forgiveness, it's important to look at temptation. Every person is tempted to sin. Each person has a different area of vulnerability to sin. The grace of Jesus is in your heart; that grace is the path that God gives to escape sin. But without God, a person has no idea there is a possible escape and falls into a pattern of sinning. Make this truth a part of your healing. Relate it to your past and those who hurt you.

> "No temptation has seized you except what is common to man. And God is faithful; He will not let you to be tempted beyond what you can bear. But when you are tempted, He will also provide a way out so that you can stand up under it." **1 Corinthians 10:13**

**Write about the sin of those who hurt you from their perspective of being tempted with no way out.**

207. Be thankful that Christ has made a way for you to live a life that is free from the depravity of sin. Christ helps you to deal with sin and the temptation to sin as it comes up. You are fully alive in Christ, living the abundant life of healing and growth in His grace and power. Perhaps you have had to deal with harsh feelings about your past and those who hurt you. In Christ, healing means placing even those feelings at the feet of the cross, allowing Christ to take the brunt of your hurt and sorrow. Jesus died that you might live abundantly, without the past incapacitating your joy in Him.

> "In the same way, count yourselves dead to sin but alive to God in Christ Jesus." **Romans 6:11**

**Write about laying difficult feelings at the cross of your Savior.**

208. There is a level of anger that begins to choke and squeeze your spirit. It begins when your focus is taken off the Lord and put on yourself and those who hurt you. If you allow your thoughts to remain on the pain, deep-seated anger and even rage will take over your life. It is this consuming anger the Lord admonishes you to avoid. Righteous anger keeps the focus on God and releases to Him the divine judgment for wrath. Put your hope in the Lord for all that you need. He will help you keep the focus of your life on Him. A part of forgiveness is releasing the focus of deep anger to Christ.

> "Refrain from anger and turn from wrath; do not fret—it leads only to evil. For evil men will be cut off, but those who hope in the Lord will inherit the land."
>
> **Psalm 37:8,9**

**Write about your need to turn this kind of anger over to the Lord.**

____________________________________________________________

____________________________________________________________

____________________________________________________________

____________________________________________________________

____________________________________________________________

____________________________________________________________

____________________________________________________________

____________________________________________________________

____________________________________________________________

____________________________________________________________

209. It is not humanly possible to pay someone back for the wrong that was done to you. Any payback would only bring more evil and suffering into an awful situation. A huge step in forgiveness is releasing those who hurt you from your own desire to pay them back for the wrong they've done to you. When you make the decision to forgive, then your focus will easily be on the Lord. The Lord God will judge every person by what is in his or her heart and by their actions. The wrong that cannot be avenged here on earth will be divinely judged.

> "Do not say, 'I'll pay back for this wrong!' Wait for the Lord, and He will deliver you." **Proverbs 20:22**

**Write about removing yourself as judge.**

210. Take a few moments to reflect on the grace in your life. What would life be for you without the forgiveness God offers through Christ? The miracle is that the Almighty God looks at you through the shed blood of Christ and sees you as innocent and pure. It is then possible for you to see others through the righteous and loving heart that Christ Jesus has given to you. You can get rid of the awful emotions that held you captive to your past. Because of Christ's love for you, you now have the capacity to forgive and love others.

> "Get rid of all bitterness, rage and anger, brawling and slander, along with every form of malice. Be kind and compassionate to one another, forgiving each other, just as in Christ God forgave you." **Ephesians 4:31,32**

**Write about allowing the love of Christ to flow through you in forgiveness.**

___

___

___

___

___

___

___

___

___

___

211. Understanding, even just a little bit, the power God has in this universe and in your life is the beginning of awe, or holy fear. The thought of a record of every sin brings you to the end of yourself, aware that you are in desperate need of the Savior. With the wonderful grace of Christ, who paid the penalty for *all* sin, there is forgiveness possible for *all* sin. If Christ has paid the penalty even for the sins that were committed against you, and you live now in the love of Christ, there is no basis for not forgiving the one who hurt you.

> "If you, O Lord, kept a record of sins, O Lord, who could stand? But with you there is forgiveness; therefore you are feared." **Psalm 130:3,4**

**Write how this truth can transform you life.**

212. God has allowed you to have the freedom to choose. Each day is a renewed opportunity to live with the grace and love of the Lord Jesus Christ flowing through you. Continue to choose life and forgiveness and love. The blessings that God gives to you are beyond description. You will live a life of abundant, fruitful love, a life filled with grace. Your past will still be there, but the sting will be gone. The memories may try to haunt you, but the grace of the Lord Jesus will bathe them in His love for you.

> "This day I call Heaven and Earth as witnesses against you that I have set before you life and death, blessings and curses. Now choose life, so that you and your children may live." **Deuteronomy 30:19**

**Using art or artistic lettering, illustrate about choosing life, love, and forgiveness.**

213. Over and over in the Scriptures, the Lord encourages you to not strive for revenge, but to leave it to His divine judgment. Ultimately, all sin is against God; often it hurts others too. It is His place to avenge the hurt that caused you to suffer so much. By forgiving, you are removing yourself from the situation and are free to live in the grace of Christ. It may seem like a paradox: it still happened, yet your spirit is free. Through forgiveness and grace, you can live a life of peace and joy.

> "Do not take revenge, my friends, but leave room for God's wrath, for it is written: 'It is mine to avenge; I will repay,' says the Lord." **Romans 12:19**

**Write about your feelings, of being released from anger and living in peace.**

214. The Lord sees what is right for you. He will help you, as you put your trust in Him. Ask the Lord to show you what is right for you, personally. Follow the Holy Spirit's prompting in your spirit. Forgiving those who hurt you opens the door of your heart to the righteousness of living in the grace and peace of Christ. Trusting God to take care of all that was wrong takes the pressure and the guilt off yourself. You were not able to fix the hurt and now you need to forgive yourself as well as those who hurt you.

> "May my vindication come from you; may your eyes see what is right." **Psalm 17:2**

**Write about trusting God with all that was wrong and learning all that is right in the Presence of God.**

215. There are many people who refuse the truth of the Gospel of Christ. The wicked things they do and the way they hurt others are an outward sign of the hardness of their hearts. A part of forgiveness involves a genuine grieving for what was done to you and for the souls who did it. They need Christ and His truth and love in their lives. This may not be possible on your own. But in the power and grace and love of Christ, it is very possible! Ask the Lord to give you His love for those you need to reach out to in forgiveness.

> "They perish because they refused to love the truth and so be saved." **2 Thessalonians 2:10b**

**Write about the grieving you feel.**

___

___

___

___

___

___

___

___

___

___

___

216. It is very easy to fall into a pattern of demanding justice from an imperfect earthly system of justice. In some situations it may seem to work, but too often those who oppress and violate others are not held accountable here on earth. When you take your plea for justice before the Holy God, you can trust completely that true justice will be the eternal answer. When you put your trust in people, you will sometimes be hurt, or disappointed. When you put your trust in the God of the universe, you will know that His justice is sure. Your spirit will be filled with His grace and love.

> "Many seek an audience with a ruler, but it is from the Lord that man gets justice." **Proverbs 29:26**

**Write about trusting God with your difficult questions.**

________________________________________________

________________________________________________

________________________________________________

________________________________________________

________________________________________________

________________________________________________

________________________________________________

________________________________________________

________________________________________________

________________________________________________

________________________________________________

217. King David wrote this prayer seeking God's wisdom for his kingdom. As in many places in the Scriptures, it also points directly to Christ Jesus. Just as Christ fulfills the prayer of David, He fulfills the prayer of your heart for righteousness and justice. The love Christ Jesus has for you is deep with compassion. His justice is a promise, as solid as the foundations of the universe that He continually holds in place. He is the Royal Son, your King, and He loves you.

> "Endow the King with your justice, O God, The Royal Son with your righteousness. He will judge your people in righteousness, your afflicted ones with justice."
>
> **Psalm 72:1,2**

**Write about receiving His promise of justice.**

218. The Lord Jesus gives very strong direction for forgiving those who hurt you. Peter asked a very reasonable question: should he forgive even if the same offense is done repeatedly? Biblical scholars explain the answer Jesus gave as forgiving so many times that it is without number. It is hard to even ponder this on the human level. It is made possible by the grace that Christ Jesus brings to your heart. Keep your focus on Jesus, that He died for every person, every sin. He made the way for forgiveness.

> "Then Peter came to Jesus and asked, 'Lord, how many times shall I forgive my brother when he sins against me? Up to seven times?' Jesus answered, 'I tell you, not seven times, but seventy seven times.' " **Matthew 18:21,22**

**Write about one person, the wrong that Christ has covered and the grace He is giving you to forgive.**

219. Contemplate the deep truth and the wisdom of God that this verse reveals. All sin is against God first. Christ Jesus paid the awful price for all sin to be forgiven. If you hold onto that which He has already forgiven, you are then sinning against the Lord. You would be refusing to allow a person's sins to be forgiven, thereby putting yourself up as the ultimate judge. If you were to remain unrepentant of that sin, how would the Lord forgive you?

> "For if you forgive men when they sin against you, your Heavenly Father will also forgive you. But if you do not forgive men their sins, your Father will not forgive your sins." **Matthew 6:14,15**

**Forgiveness is allowing another's sin to be between that person and God, rather than that person and you. Write about this truth in your life.**

220. What a wonderful thing it is to be loved by God! He longs to be gracious to you, to fill your life with His grace. At the core of forgiveness is a compassion that is immeasurable because it comes from God. He shows you His compassion through His Word and His love for you. The Lord God, in His divine compassion, fills you with grace. When you receive that grace, you also share His grace, love, and forgiveness with others.

> "Yet the Lord longs to be gracious to you; He rises to show you compassion. For the Lord is a God of justice. Blessed are all who wait for Him!" **Isaiah 30:18**

**Write about His compassion, grace, and forgiveness in your life.**

221. The Lord conveys a model of true justice for His people. Mercy and compassion lead the way to living at peace with yourself and with others. Forgiveness is releasing evil thoughts about someone else from your heart and soul. This is so freeing to your spirit! It releases you from the constraints of your past to be the person God has intended you to be.

> "This is what the Lord Almighty says: 'Administer true justice; show mercy and compassion to one another. In your hearts do not think evil of each other.'"
>
> **Zechariah 7:9,10b**

**Write how beginning to live in true justice has changed your life.**

___________________________________________

___________________________________________

___________________________________________

___________________________________________

___________________________________________

___________________________________________

___________________________________________

___________________________________________

___________________________________________

___________________________________________

___________________________________________

222. You may have felt overwhelmed by the hurt of your past. The effect of such deep trauma is devastating. God does not want you to live in such pain, but rather in His abundance. When you focus on the pain and those who hurt you, you can be overcome by evil through an unforgiving heart. The Lord calls you to overcome evil with good. Compassion and forgiveness, for yourself and for others in your past, will break the cycle of being overwhelmed by the pain.

> "Do not be overcome by evil, but overcome evil with good." **Romans 12:21**

**Write about seeking the compassion and forgiveness of Christ and His goodness to help you overcome evil.**

223. Forgiveness is a daily choice to follow Christ and seek His grace in your life. If you struggle with it, but have a heart that desires the Lord's compassion to flow through you, He will help you. You need to be careful of allowing your heart to become self-focused and open to sin. It creeps in so easily. If sin starts rearing its ugly head, recognize it, seek the forgiving grace of Christ and allow Christ to cleanse your heart. Keep your heart seeking after the love of the Lord Jesus.

> "If we deliberately keep on sinning after we have received the knowledge of the truth, no sacrifice for sins is left, but only a fearful expectation of judgment and of raging fire that will consume the enemies of God."
>
> **Hebrews 10:26,27**

**Write about choosing a life of forgiveness rather than sin.**

224. When you were hurt, you fought in your heart, mind, and even in your body — the wrongness of what happened to you. Your natural inclination was to try any way possible to protect yourself and then to condemn those who were involved. Life in Christ turns all the natural inclinations upside-down. Jesus encourages you to understand that every person has sinned before the holiness of God and therefore is equal in sin. In forgiveness, your individual condemnation of another is removed and God is allowed to work His miracle of grace in your life.

> "Do not judge, and you will not be judged. Do not condemn, and you will not be condemned. Forgive, and you will be forgiven." **Luke 6:37**

**Write about freeing up your spirit, so that God can work His miracle of healing in you.**

______________________________________________

______________________________________________

______________________________________________

______________________________________________

______________________________________________

______________________________________________

______________________________________________

______________________________________________

______________________________________________

______________________________________________

225. Living the Christian life is energized by an active faith. This involves being willing to face the most difficult things with the love Christ has given you. You may have a whole list of grievances against those who hurt you when you were so vulnerable. Through the grace of Christ, you are given the power to release all of them. You may still be sad about the whole situation, but again, the love and grace of Christ will cover you in peace.

> "Bear with each other and forgive whatever grievances you may have against one another. Forgive as the Lord forgave you." **Colossians 3:13**

**Write about living an active faith of forgiveness.**

___

___

___

___

___

___

___

___

___

___

___

226. Suffering deals such a blow to your spirit that often all emotions are felt more intensely. You may have even backed away from your emotions to avoid what seemed to be hyper-emotional responses. Through the healing power of Christ Jesus, kindness, compassion and forgiveness can be felt and embraced as a new way of life. Even the peace of living in Christ, with all of the burden of the past lifted from you, can be felt more profoundly and appreciated with all that is in you.

> "Be kind and compassionate to one another, forgiving each other, just as in Christ God forgave you."
>
> **Ephesians 4:32**

**Write about the intensity of the emotions in your life, during the trauma and now, living in the grace of Christ.**

227. There is something about trauma that is so devastating to the soul. Satan uses the sin, which someone has chosen, to twist lies into your spirit. A part of the work of grace that Christ brings to your spirit is to untwist the jumble of lies and speak His truth of love into your life. You have been set free from the consuming hurt of your past. Now your heart and soul and spirit is filled with the gracious love of God and His righteousness. Your hope is for His love to grow within you and overflow to others.

> "You have been set free from sin and have become slaves to righteousness." **Romans 6:18**

**Write about the joy of living for the righteousness of God.**

228. God gives you a wonderful promise, that your deep prayer for your healing will be fulfilled. He provides a pattern for prayer, first, asking and second, believing that you will receive it. The third portion of the Lord blessing your prayer is forgiveness. When you forgive others, your heart is cleansed from all thoughts and feelings that could lead to sin. Your heart is open to the love of Christ and the prompting of the Holy Spirit.

> "Therefore I tell you, whatever you ask for in prayer, believe that you have received it, and it will be yours. And when you stand praying, if you hold anything against anyone, forgive him, so that your Father in Heaven may forgive your sins." **Mark 11:24,25**

**Write about forgiveness and God's promise of answered prayer.**

229. From the time of your trauma until the beginning of genuine healing in Christ, you may have felt immobilized emotionally by fear, rage and bitterness. Satan used these emotions and your hurt and confusion to keep you stuck in the evil situation. With the healing grace of Christ, you no longer have to remain there. Forgiveness releases all of those unhealthy emotions. You are now free to offer your life fully to God, for His work of righteousness.

> "Do not offer the parts of your body to sin, as instruments of wickedness, but rather offer yourselves to God, as those who have been brought from death to life; and offer the parts of your body to Him as instruments of righteousness." **Romans 6:13**

**Write about offering to God your mind and body for righteousness.**

___

___

___

___

___

___

___

___

___

___

230. Your life touches so many people. By living each day in the grace of the Lord, you are blessing others. Forgiveness is a choice to make each day, a choice to live by the power of the Holy Spirit working through you in love. Do not allow even one day of bitterness to ruin your joy in Christ. Bitterness spreads too quickly to others and will cause trouble and defilement. God made you to be an example for others. Just by continuing to keep your heart pure before the Lord, you are able to bless others with the grace of God. What a wonderful truth!

> "See to it that no one misses the grace of God and that no bitter root grows up to cause trouble and defile many."
>
> **Hebrews 12:15**

**Write about your heart for others, that your life might be a source of the Lord's grace flowing to them.**

231. Forgiveness in Christ is so filled with His grace that miracles are possible. The biggest miracle is that through the great love of the Savior, you are enabled to not only forgive, but also to seek the Lord's blessing for those who hurt you. You are able to see their pain and their need of the Lord's grace. Take a few moments to go before the Lord and ask for His blessings to flow upon each individual involved in the hurt of your past.

> "Do not repay evil or insult with insult, but with blessing, because to this you were called so that you may inherit a blessing." **Peter 3:9**

**Write how you feel after such miracle prayer.**

232. The love that Jesus has for you is so intense and powerful! He gave His life for your healing and restoration. That same love flows through your spirit, by the indwelling power of the Holy Spirit. Allow the fullness of that love to bear fruit in your daily life. Be open to opportunities that God will give you to lay your life down for others, whether in service or encouragement. Allow forgiveness to be so complete, that you are able to pray for even those who have hurt you. Be active in your walk with the Lord, seeking ways you can give your life for people in your past and your present.

> "This is how we know what love is: Jesus Christ laid down His life for us. And we ought to lay down our lives for our brothers." **1 John 3:16**

**Write about knowing that you have forgiven, by His love and grace.**

________________________________________________

________________________________________________

________________________________________________

________________________________________________

________________________________________________

________________________________________________

________________________________________________

________________________________________________

________________________________________________

________________________________________________

233. A very sad aspect of life is the realization that some people will not receive the forgiveness you offer. They have the right to choose to reject you and stay in sin, ultimately rejecting God. When this happens, it seems to hurt you all over again. The only thing that you can do is seek God's grace in your life and make the effort to be at peace with them. Continue to seek holiness through Jesus' grace in your life. Seek God's wisdom to lead your feelings and prayer for those who reject your sincere outreach of love.

> "Make every effort to live in peace with all men and to be holy; without holiness no one will see the Lord."
>
> **Hebrews 12:14**

**Write about making every effort to live in peace.**

___

___

___

___

___

___

___

___

___

___

___

234. There are those who believe peace means never dealing with difficult issues. It is very easy to smooth over a problem and "keep the peace." When this occurs, it is the first step to denial that there even is a problem. Christ calls you to a true peace, a peace based on the willingness to face issues and work through them. Divine grace enables you to recognize a problem, forgive the person involved, and be healed of the pain of that incident. Reconciliation and a peace based on truth is then possible.

> "If it is possible, as far as it depends on you, live at peace with everyone." **Romans 12:18**

**Write about living in true peace.**

235. When you were stuck with so much pain in your heart, the unforgiveness created a blockage in your relationship with God. By choosing to forgive those who hurt you, the blockage is being removed and cleansed. You are able to draw near to God with a sincere heart. Each part of this verse is true because you have chosen forgiveness. You are being cleansed from all bitterness. You are free to have an ever-deepening relationship with the Father God, the Savior, and the comforting Holy Spirit.

> "Let us draw near to God with a sincere heart in full assurance of faith, having our hearts sprinkled to cleanse us from a guilty conscience and having our bodies washed with pure water." **Hebrews 10:22**

**Write about drawing near to God.**

236. The Word of God inspires believers to always seek the Lord and His holiness. You have sought the Lord throughout the process of healing, focusing on His power to heal the hurt. You have put a huge effort into seeking divine healing and grace in your life. You have taken difficult steps and have been given grace for these steps in the healing process. Remember to keep yourself in God's love. If Satan tries to throw the old hurt at you, or anger or bitterness about it, seek the Lord's love to cover you in grace.

> "Keep yourselves in God's love as you wait for the mercy of our Lord Jesus Christ to bring you to eternal life."
>
> **Jude 21**

**Write about living in God's love.**

___

___

___

___

___

___

___

___

___

___

___

237. God's love lives in you. Following His direction for healing is making that love complete. He desires victory for you, victory over the awful stuff you lived through. The power of His grace shows in your life. Forgiveness has been possible only by the grace of Christ Jesus in your life. You are His joy because you have chosen His path of love. You will be a witness to others of the depth of God's love. You are a witness of His love in this world because you are like Him; you live in His grace.

> "God is love. Whoever lives in love lives in God, and God in him. In this way, love is made complete among us so that we will have confidence on the day of judgment, because in this world we are like Him." **1 John 4:16b,17**

**Write about God's love in you.**

238. Experiencing God's love is like being at a huge family picnic. Hugs all around—from generation to generation, love flows. Tiny babies are cooed over; youngsters run and play with joyful abandon. Favorite dishes are gobbled up, their recipes shared. Sweet memories are reminisced and cherished. The love of a family is given and received a hundred times over. God's love is like this, very rich in dimension and depth. His grace and compassion is always available for those who desire Him. His righteous anger is there for a boundary. He is slow to bring it to bear, making every opportunity for grace.

> "The Lord is gracious and compassionate, slow to anger and rich in love." **Psalm 145:8**

**Write about the richness of God's love in your life.**

___

___

___

___

___

___

___

___

___

___

239. As you walk through the aspects of forgiveness, you are passing from a living death, filled with bitterness and rage, to eternal life in Christ. It is by learning and experiencing the love of Christ that you are able to forgive. The Holy Spirit fills your spirit with divine compassion which extends even to those who hurt you so much. By the love of God, you have been set free from your past. You have followed the example of the Lord Jesus, who loved so completely He was able to forgive.

> "We know that we have passed from death to life, because we love our brothers. Anyone who does not love remains in death." **1 John 3:14**

**Write how the love of Christ has changed you and given you new life.**

240. In Christ, you have been forgiven of all your sins. You have given Him your pain, confusion, and sorrow. You have learned to forgive in His Name. When you were stuck in Satan's grip of pain from your trauma, you may have done something that brings horrible shame to your conscience, even now as you recall the memory of it. Trust in Christ to cleanse your conscience from any act that you did that would lead to death in your spirit. Forgive yourself as He forgives you. With His divine cleansing, you are free to serve Him in joy, peace, and love.

> "How much more, then, will the blood of Christ, who through the eternal Spirit offered Himself unblemished to God, cleanse our consciences from acts that lead to death, so that we may serve the living God!"
>
> **Hebrews 9:14**

**Write about Jesus' cleansing of your soul and forgiving yourself.**

______________________________________________

______________________________________________

______________________________________________

______________________________________________

______________________________________________

______________________________________________

______________________________________________

______________________________________________

______________________________________________

241. God was pleased to have salvation made possible through Christ Jesus. He was pleased to bring a Holy peace by the shedding of Jesus' blood on the cross. God is pleased that you have come to peace, that you have chosen to forgive. He has been with you, loving you and healing your wounded spirit. He is pleased that you are filled with the love of Christ. You are a part of the fullness that dwells in Christ — a beloved child of the Father God.

> "For God was pleased to have all His fullness dwell in Him, and through Him to reconcile to Himself all things, whether things on Earth or things in Heaven, by making peace through His blood, shed on the cross."
>
> **Colossians 1:19,20**

**Write how your life has changed since beginning this journey of healing.**

___

___

___

___

___

___

___

___

___

___

242. You have been given the light of Christ to dispel the darkness of your suffering. Through Christ, you are made righteous. He has placed in you grace and compassion. You have victory and healing because of all Christ has brought to your life. You have followed Him in compassion and forgiveness. Christ Jesus is your light.

> "Even in darkness light dawns for the upright, for the gracious and compassionate and righteous man."
>
> **Psalm 112:4**

**Write a prayer of thankfulness for your life in Him. After writing, take a few moments to praise Him for bringing His light of love into what was your darkness.**

243. You are a peacemaker; you have learned the transforming power of forgiveness. The Lord has done a work of grace in you. The bitterness has been released from your spirit. People have been released from your past. Prayerful compassion has gone before them, seeking the will of Christ for each individual. You have sown peace. You will raise from this a harvest of righteousness. Your choice to be a peacemaker touches many lives with the grace of the Lord.

> "Peacemakers who sow in peace raise a harvest of righteousness." **James 3:18**

**Write about being a peacemaker.**

# Chapter 5: Your Identity in Christ, Rather than Victimization

In this chapter, you will be able to explore how your identity is in Christ, rather than identifying with the abuse and trauma that you experienced. The beauty of the flame, symbolizing the majesty of God, reflects the miracle of your righteousness in Christ. Receive your true identity, deeply rooted in the Lord God.

244. You may have felt that part of your identity has been defined by the trauma or abuse you suffered. Emotional pain is very subtle. It can become a part of your life so much that one of the ways you think of yourself is as a victim. The next step in this intense healing process is to begin to recognize your identity in Christ Jesus, rather than in victimization. He has set you free from the emotional pain. Your identity is defined in grace.

> "Therefore, there is now no condemnation for those who are in Christ Jesus, because through Christ Jesus the law of the Spirit of life set me free from the law of sin and death." **Romans 8:1,2**

**Write about being a victim too long and your desire to have your identity fully in Christ.**

___

___

___

___

___

___

___

___

___

___

245. You have lived through so much wickedness. You may have felt almost strangled by the cords of the past wrapping tightly around you. Christ the Lord has cut those cords and set you free from them. Though you may always be aware of the bruising that occurred in your life, you are no longer bound in the captivity of the trauma. The spirit that the Lord Jesus created in you is free to grow and become all that He has planned for you. Healing is a work of righteousness that the Lord is doing in your spirit. You are being blessed.

> "But the Lord is righteous; He has cut me free from the cords of the wicked." **Psalm 129:4**

**Write about your feelings of your freedom in Christ.**

________________________________________________

________________________________________________

________________________________________________

________________________________________________

________________________________________________

________________________________________________

________________________________________________

________________________________________________

________________________________________________

________________________________________________

________________________________________________

246. The Lord has turned your darkness into the gracious light of His love. He will keep you in that light. Your identity is in Christ. His Spirit will keep the lamp of your soul burning in the love of Christ. This may be such a new experience for you that it may be a bit overwhelming. Take the time you need to rest in your new identity in Christ Jesus. There will begin to grow in your mind, body, and spirit a deep, profound joy.

> "You, O Lord, keep my lamp burning; my God turns my darkness into light. **Psalm 18:28**

**Write how you feel living every moment in the grace of Jesus' love.**

247. As your identity is more and more in Christ, you will find it easier to set aside evil thoughts and do the good things of the Lord. Satan will not have the pull he once had on you. Each day, place your identity fully in Christ, rather than in the victimization that once defined you as a person. Remind yourself throughout the day, that you are a child of the King. Pursue the peace of the Living Lord.

"Turn from evil and do good; seek peace and pursue it."

**Psalm 34:14**

**Write about getting used to the new you!**

248. With Christ, you have a strength that is beyond your humanity. Because of His Presence in your life, you are able to accomplish things you have never imagined. Your hope is in the King of all kings, who loves you and blesses you. Rest in this wonderful identity that is yours, Christ in you and you in Him. Trust in the strength He is giving you. There is a purpose in this strength. You will be strong in the power of His mighty Name, for His blessing in your life and in the lives of many others.

"Be strong and take heart, all you who hope in the Lord."
**Psalm 31:24**

**Write about the Lord's strength in your new life of healing.**

249. The Lord Jesus brought you to Himself for your salvation. He has also brought you near to Himself through the healing of your soul and spirit. Not only do you feel nearer to the Lord, since there are no barriers of painful emotions, but the fact is, you are nearer to Him. Your spirit is open to the gentle, prompting of the Holy Spirit. You are now able to experience the profound joy of being very near the Savior. Your identity is delightfully becoming less about you and more about Christ in you.

> "But now in Christ Jesus you who once were far away have been brought near through the blood of Christ."
>
> **Ephesians 2:13**

**Write about being near the Lord Jesus Christ.**

250. Your life was stuck in the pit of suffering. The Lord Jesus redeemed you from that horrible life. Remember what He has done for you and appreciate your life in His grace. The compassion of the Lord overflows from His Spirit to yours, crowning you with divine compassion to bless others in His Name. What an honor it is to be crowned with compassion!

> "Praise the Lord, who redeems your life from the pit and crowns you with love and compassion." **Psalm 103:1a,4**

**Write about how you feel, that you have been given such love.**

251. The Lord has been your strength and shield throughout your life. He has helped to bring you to a place of healing. You have learned to put your entire life before Him in complete trust of His love for you. As you realize how much your life has changed, allow the joy to fill the day with thanksgiving. You are no longer that person who continually lived in the moment of suffering, long after the event had passed. You are a glorious child of the King. His glory shines through you.

> "The Lord is my strength and my shield; my heart trusts in Him, and I am helped. My heart leaps for joy and I will give thanks to Him in song." **Psalm 28:7**

**Add your note of joy, after singing:**
**'Thank you Lord for saving my soul, thank you Lord for making me whole.**
**Thank you Lord for giving to me—thy great salvation so rich and free.'**

______________________________________________

______________________________________________

______________________________________________

______________________________________________

______________________________________________

______________________________________________

______________________________________________

______________________________________________

______________________________________________

252. Explore the love that you have for God. It has been there since the moment you accepted the Lord Jesus into your heart. He lifted from you the burden of sin and through the power of His Word, the hurt of your past. Now you are free to experience His love for you and your love for Him. Rest in the quietness of a moment with the God of the universe. Allow your love for Him to seep into your body and every unseen place of your soul.

> "Love the Lord your God with all your heart and with all your soul and with all your strength." **Deuteronomy 6:5**

**Write of your love for the Father God, your Lord and Savior Jesus, and the Holy Spirit, your Comforter and Guide.**

___________________________________________

___________________________________________

___________________________________________

___________________________________________

___________________________________________

___________________________________________

___________________________________________

___________________________________________

___________________________________________

___________________________________________

___________________________________________

253. Many things of Christ seem like complex paradoxes. One aspect of your identity in Christ is that you were chosen according to His plan of grace. He rejoices to give you the healing you have desired. The divine purpose He has for you will be accomplished. In love and grace He chose you. Even though you may not fully understand what it is to be predestined for God's purpose, receive the joy of being called of the Lord. He has loved you from before creation.

> "In Him we were also chosen, having been predestined according to the plan of Him who works out everything in conformity with the purpose of His will."
>
> **Ephesians 1:11**

**Write about being chosen in the love and grace of Christ.**

254. Another paradox of faith in Christ Jesus is that you carry in your body the death of the Savior. It was a gift for you that He died, removing the penalty of your sin. When you received that gift, not only was your soul cleansed, but you also received the imprint of the Savior's death. With the immense power of the resurrection, the everlasting life of Christ is declared in you. The part of you that truly was a victim was put to death in Christ. The resurrection power of Christ is your real identity, His life is revealed in yours.

> "We always carry around in our body the death of Jesus, so that the life of Jesus may also be revealed in our body."
>
> **2 Corinthians 4:10**

**Write about how you feel that Christ is revealed in you.**

255. Christ the Lord has changed every part of your life. Your body was broken and dishonored; Christ has healed the wounds and will give you a wonderful, perfect spiritual body. You were once weak and now you are full of strength and power because of the grace of Christ. Your personal identity is no longer limited to that which was hurt. You have been given resurrection power for your body, as well as for your spirit. Your identity is intertwined with Christ; He is working a divine purpose in your life. Take time to consider the immensity of your body being raised in glory.

> "The body that is sown is perishable, it is raised imperishable; it is sown in dishonor, it is raised in glory; it is sown in weakness, it is raised in power; it is sown a natural body, it is raised a spiritual body."
>
> **1 Corinthians 15:42b-44**

**Write how this changes your perception of your body.**

________________________________________

________________________________________

________________________________________

________________________________________

________________________________________

________________________________________

________________________________________

________________________________________

________________________________________

256. One day Jesus will transform your body to be like His glorious body. You will be prepared to live in Heaven, where you really have citizenship. It is right that you should eagerly await such awonderful experience. Your glorified body will not carry the burden of the pain you have suffered. Always look forward to that final step of healing. Recognize that the body you have now does carrythe memory of what you suffered. Take time to care for your body,using lotion to caress areas that were hurt. Honor the body God has given you for now, keeping in your heart the hope for a body glorified in the power of Jesus.

> "But our citizenship is in Heaven. And we eagerly await a Savior from there, the Lord Jesus Christ, who by the power that enables Him to bring everything under His control, will transform our lowly bodies so that they will be like His glorious body." **Philippians 3:20,21**

**Write about caring for your body.**

257. By having faith in Christ Jesus, your life has been changed. By the power of His Word, you have been healed of the woundedness you had lived with. Through worship, your identity in Christ is truly experienced. Worship is more than singing and praying, It is giving your body, each day, all day long, as a living sacrifice to God. Allow your body to be used to honor the Lord. It is no longer an instrument of the past, bearing the trauma of the past. It is an instrument of holiness before the Lord.

> "Therefore, I urge you brothers, in view of God's mercy, to offer your bodies as living sacrifices, holy and pleasing to God—this is your spiritual act of worship." **Romans 12:1**

**Write about offering your body in worship to God.**

258. You have been set free from sin and the pain of victimization. You have chosen to be a slave to the holiness of God, rather than to the evil of Satan. It is your choice, in the most rewarding kind of service, to give your life willingly to Christ. God's holiness will be displayed in your life because of His grace. Each day, your heart is more in tune with the Holy Spirit. Because you are willing to be a slave to God and His purpose in your life, God will allow His holiness to shine through you. Your identity is caught up in Him. What a wonderful place to be!

> "But now that you have been set free from sin and have become slaves to God, the benefit you reap leads to holiness, and the result is eternal life." **Romans 6:22**

**Write about being a slave to God, for His work of grace.**

259. The grace of salvation and healing was given through Jesus Christ to you. It is a grace that has no measure of time and no boundary of blessing in your life. It is essential to acknowledge that your identity in Christ is entirely by His grace. It is not based on what happened to you in the past, nor what you accomplish in your present or future. By living in grace and embracing your true identity in Christ, you open the door for God's blessing of holiness in your life.

> "God, who has saved us and called us to a holy life — not because of anything we have done but because of His own purpose and grace. This grace was given us in Christ Jesus before the beginning of time." **2 Timothy 1:8c,9**

**Make a list of the ways that the grace of Jesus Christ has changed your life.**

260. Through the ministry of the Holy Spirit, holy wisdom and strength are given to you. Throughout the day and even into the night, the Spirit of the Lord is your Counselor. This is only the beginning of your life in the Presence of God. Be thankful for His wisdom. Follow His gentle leading. Praise His Holy Name! Rest in His Presence. Cherish the reality of His daily counsel and love.

> "I will praise the Lord, who counsels me; even at night my heart instructs me." **Psalm 16:7**

**Write a prayer of joy.**

261. The darkness you once lived in now seems like a bad dream. The memory of it lingers, but it has no tangible hold on you. Your life now is full of the light of Christ Jesus. You have been blessed with healing. Live each day with righteousness and truth bringing joy to your spirit. You are a child of light; the goodness of Christ will shine forth from your emotions and actions.

> "For you were once darkness, but now you are light in the Lord. Live as children of light (for the fruit of the light consists in all goodness, righteousness and truth)."
>
> **Ephesians 5:8,9**

**Describe your life as a child of light, with the darkness banished in the grace of Christ.**

262. As you grow in Christ, lean on His Spirit to guide you. The Word is wisdom to your life, to your spirit; soak in its truths. As the Lord guides you, follow His will. Give honor and praise to the Trinity of love, the Father, Son, and Spirit. Embrace His love in your life and in your relationships. Each day, affirm your identity as one who is righteous through the grace of Jesus Christ.

> "Teach me to do your will, for you are my God; may your good Spirit lead me on level ground." **Psalm 143:10**

**Write how your relationship with God has deepened in this season of healing.**

263. The Lord Jesus is your rock and your fortress. He is a sure place of healing, righteousness, love, and grace. Your healing has brought honor and glory to His Name. As you follow His direction for your life, He will bless others through the unique gifting He has placed in you. His Name will again be lifted up in honor and glory. Take a moment to thank God in prayer and seek His guidance.

> "Since you are my rock and my fortress, for the sake of your Name lead me and guide me." **Psalm 31:3**

**Write about who you are in Jesus and your desire to honor His Name.**

264. Sin and suffering are based on the lies of Satan. For too long, you lived under the direct influence of his lies. A foundational part of your healing is that you have secured The Truth, which is Jesus Christ, in your life. It is by the grace and love of Jesus that His truth has banished the lies of your past. Continue to be open to the Holy truths of God. Place your hope in Him and nothing else.

> "Guide me in your truth and teach me, for you are my God and my Savior, and my hope is in you all day long."
>
> **Psalm 25:5**

**Write about living in truth.**

265. Your heart was so burdened when you were in the midst of suffering. The Lord Jesus has changed all that for you, by setting your heart free in His grace. You are free to run in the joy of His righteousness. He will give you a path, one that is perfect for you and blesses you. In His path of joy, you will bless others as well, and bring honor to His Name.

> "I run in the path of your commands, for you have set my heart free." **Psalm 119:32**

**Write about running free, either physically, emotionally, or spiritually, in the freedom of the Lord's grace and love.**

266. You no longer have to be consumed with emotional trauma from the past. Through the grace and power of the Word of God, you have died to the suffering of your past. Your life is now hidden with Christ in God. You are surrounded by the mystery and majesty of the Holy God. You are given a peace that meets the deepest need of your soul. Allow your thoughts to be guided by the Holy Spirit. Think about things of Heaven, of the glory of God and ofHis love for you.

> "Set your minds on things above, not on earthly things. For you died, and your life is now hidden with Christ in God." **Colossians 3:2,3**

**Write about being hidden with Christ in God.**

______________________________________________

______________________________________________

______________________________________________

______________________________________________

______________________________________________

______________________________________________

______________________________________________

______________________________________________

______________________________________________

______________________________________________

______________________________________________

267. Victimizing thoughts may have kept you in depression for years. Satan will use thoughts to try to keep you immobilized in emotional pain. A significant step of healing is to identify patterns of thinking that are destructive emotionally and to learn to think in a more uplifting way. Ask the Holy Spirit to help you replace any negative thought with things that will bless your mind and your spirit.

> "Finally, brothers, whatever is true, whatever is noble, whatever is right, whatever is pure, whatever is lovely, whatever is admirable—if anything is excellent or praise-worthy—think about such things." **Philippians 4:8**

**Identify and list thoughts that are painful. Then list the truths about God's love for you.**

268. Perhaps people have said to you, "Let the past go." It is very difficult to do so when the past affects you in the present. The Lord has taken you through a journey of healing by His Word of love and grace. The past no longer has a tight grip on your life. You are able to release it and even forget it in the grace of Christ. The goal of what lies ahead is so glorious that what is past is like a dull dream of what once was. Direct your energy and your interest to focus on your life in Christ. Seek the Lord and His will for your life.

> "Forgetting what is behind and straining toward what is ahead, I press on toward the goal to win the prize for which God has called me heavenward in Christ Jesus."
>
> **Philippians 3:13b,14**

**Write about forgetting what is past and living for what is ahead in Christ.**

269. You have been given a personal miracle, a holy cleansing of the pain that once tormented your spirit. Release the old, uncomfortable life of pain and put on the new self that Christ has given you. In His grace, He has made you to be a reflection of God, full of compassion and righteousness. He has given you a unique perspective of suffering. You will be able to reach out in tremendous empathy and love to others who have suffered as you have. As you embrace your new identity in Christ, He will give you His vision for your life in Him.

"Put on the new self, created to be like God in true righteousness and holiness." **Ephesians 4:24b**

**Write about putting on your new self.**

270. You share, with all other believers in Jesus Christ, the holy, heavenly calling. Your ultimate hope in eternal life opens your heart to living each day in Christ. It is an exhilarating life to which you are called, even here on Earth. Each day, focus on Jesus. He is your High Priest, the One who will guide you, helping you to grow in His grace. When you place your thoughts on the majesty of Jesus, there is no room for old patterns of thinking. You are holy, becoming ever more so each day, because of the work of healing and grace that Christ Jesus is doing in you.

> "Therefore, holy brothers, who share in the heavenly calling, fix your thoughts on Jesus, the Apostle and High Priest whom we confess." **Hebrews 3:1**

**Write about choosing to think about the Lord.**

271. One of the most profound consequences of suffering is a deep hunger for the righteousness of God. You have suffered Satan's torment and have longed for an end to all suffering. Christ has healed your own personal suffering and has blessed your heart with empathy for others. Your hunger and thirst for the complete righteousness of God to be revealed continues to grow in intensity. This is His grace working in you, the Holy Spirit affirming His will in your spirit. The Lord will continue to bless you immensely as you seek His righteousness with all your heart.

> "Blessed are those who hunger and thirst for righteousness, for they will be filled." **Matthew 5:6**

**Write how your suffering has brought about such a deep hunger for God's righteousness.**

272. Jesus gave His life, so that you can be completely reconciled with God. Since you have received His gift, you have also received easy access to the God of the universe. Perhaps the concept of Father God has been perplexing because of emotional damage from your suffering. Laying aside your jumbled emotions, begin to embrace the true, loving Father God with a new trust. Go to Him anytime, with confidence of His love and compassion for you. Your identity is in being His child; you are loved with an everlasting love.

> "In Him and through faith in Him we may approach God with freedom and confidence." **Ephesians 3:12**

**Write about approaching your Father God.**

273. Christ has empowered you to follow Him in godliness. His Word has healed you from your woundedness. There once was an image of brokenness filtering all of your life. Now in Christ, there is an image of His love pouring grace into your life. Keep in His Word; learn more of His life, His compassion, and His grace. Use the power He has given you. Follow the vision the Holy Spirit affirms for your life. Jesus called you by His own glory. You are precious to Him.

> "His divine power has given us everything we need for life and godliness through our knowledge of Him who called us by His own glory and goodness." **2 Peter 1:3**

**Write about being empowered to follow Christ.**

274. Christ has given you an example of living in love, by giving Himself up for you. God honors His gift; it is a fragrant offering of love. Identify with His Spirit in you so thoroughly that you no longer consider yourself the victim you once were, but rather a beloved child of the King. Your life is a life of love, rather than the life of being a victim. Giving your life to Christ is the greatest kind of freedom, because it is being submissive to everything good. You are able to give love because the love of God is deep in your spirit.

> "Be imitators of God, therefore, as dearly loved children and live a life of love, just as Christ loved us and gave Himself up for us as a fragrant offering and sacrifice to God." **Ephesians 5:1,2**

**Write about being an imitator of God, living a life of love.**

275. Always come back to the fact of the Holy God choosing you and loving you. This is the foundation to build your life on. Each day, receive His love anew. Allow Him to clothe you with the wonderful aspects of His love, compassion, kindness, humility, gentleness, and patience. It is like wearing the love of Christ as a cozy fleece robe on a chilly winter morning. The warmth of His love seeps into your soul and allows you to give this deep, powerful love to others. It is a divine clothing, given to you in grace and love from Christ.

> "Therefore, as God's chosen people, holy and dearly loved, clothe yourselves with compassion, kindness, humility, gentleness, and patience." **Colossians 3:12**

**Write about being clothed with the love of Christ.**

276. Jesus has poured His grace into your life. In addition, believers encourage you on the marathon that is your life in Christ. You have gone through tremendous healing and are stretching out to run the race Christ has set before you. With Christ going before you, you can say "No" to negative patterns that would pull your focus again to yourself and your pain and draw your eyes away from Him. Seek the grace of Christ and His wisdom for the direction of your life. He will guide you in this race that is uniquely yours.

> "Therefore, since we are surrounded by such a great cloud of witnesses, let us throw off everything that hinders and the sin that so easily entangles, and let us run with perseverance the race marked out for us." **Hebrews 12:1**

**Describe how your life in Christ resembles a marathon.**

277. You have been made holy in Christ. Father God gives His holiness to you, in a fellowship with a family like no other. Christ Jesus is not only your Savior, but also your Brother. He is not ashamed in any way to call you brother, or sister. How different is this holy family to which you belong! To experience true holiness and the most profound fellowship is to have every need of your mind, body and spirit entirely fulfilled.

> "Both the One who makes men holy and those who are made holy are of the same family. So Jesus is not ashamed to call them brothers." **Hebrews 2:11**

**Write about your needs and how they might be fulfilled within the holy family where your identity now exists.**

___

___

___

___

___

___

___

___

___

___

___

278. As your spirit is being healed by the grace of Christ, even your body will reflect the Lord's glory. Your face no longer reflects the pain of the past; it is okay to release the pain from the control it had in your life. You are now free to express the joy of living in grace. As you seek the Lord each day, your life will be transformed to exemplify Christ. You will be filled with His righteousness, peace, integrity, love, compassion, and many other qualities that are divinely given.

> "And we, who with unveiled faces all reflect the Lord's glory, are being transformed into His likeness with ever-increasing glory, which comes from the Lord, who is the Spirit." **2 Corinthians 3:18**

**Write a prayer of thankfulness that His glory is being reflected in you.**

279. Part of the holiness of God is that He is beyond the realm of human understanding. By grace, you are able to not only follow Christ, but live in Him. A most wonderful miracle of grace is that Jesus' Spirit lives in you. There is a holy fellowship that connects you with the Father and His son, Jesus — through grace and the Presence of the Holy Spirit. Listen, as the Holy Spirit speaks His will for your life to your heart. Follow it as best you can and the way will become more and more clear to you. Live by His Word. Rejoice in the fellowship the Spirit brings to your spirit.

> "Those who obey His commands live in Him, and He in them. And this is how that we know that He lives in us: We know it by the Spirit He gave us." **1 John 3:24**

**Try to express through art, with creativity and abandon, how you feel with the fellowship of the Spirit.**

280. A part of your healing that is in Christ is stretching forth to a new self concept. Suffering alters your perception of the person you are. It keeps you victimized long after the trauma actually occurred. You have experienced so much healing. Make it a solid part of your life by allowing the Lord to give you a new sense of who you are in Him. He is building in you a work of grace, so that His glory is reflected to others through you. This is a self-image that incorporates His glory in your unique person.

> "And in Him you too are being built together to become a dwelling in which God lives by His Spirit."
>
> **Ephesians 2:22**

**Write about your new self-image.**

281. Long ago, God began a good work in your life by bringing you to Himself. He has placed in you a deep desire for His Presence in your life. He helped you survive horrible trauma and healed your broken heart, through His Word and powerful grace. He is giving you new insights each day about His love for you and His provision of grace in your life. The Lord God will continue His work of grace in your life, blessing you as you grow in Him.

> "Being confident of this, that He who began a good work in you will carry it on to completion until the day of Christ Jesus." **Philippians 1:6**

**Write something of what the Lord is putting in your heart about His continuing work of grace in your life.**

282. You have a glorious freedom in Christ. You are free from the burden of your past and the victimization of your spirit. Your entire life is defined differently now, by the grace of Christ rather than by the pain that you once lived through. Do not ever allow the old slave thoughts of your life as a victim, box you into a corner. Stand firm on the Word of God, His promises, His Presence, and His love. Do not waver or take even one step back to that old life of victimization. Hold onto the grace that Christ has given you. Take new steps of boldness in His power, with grace and love always going with you.

> "It is for freedom that Christ has set us free. Stand firm, then, and do not let yourselves be burdened again by a yoke of slavery." **Galatians 5:1**

**Write about your freedom in Christ.**

283. Jesus brings to your life integrity and compassion, to be demonstrated in leadership. He encourages you to grow in maturity by His grace. You no longer have to put up with deceit, manipulation, or unrestrained anger in your life. The fullness of life in Christ has been given to you. By His grace, you have been transformed from a victim to a victor. Begin to live your life in this new concept of yourself, by receiving this gift of fullness in Christ.

> "And you have been given fullness in Christ, who is the head over every power and authority." **Colossians 2:10**

**Write how empty you felt as a victim and how full you feel now because of the grace of Christ.**

___

___

___

___

___

___

___

___

___

___

___

284. The Holy Spirit, through His work of grace, enlightens your heart to the truths of God. There is a hope in Christ that is both deeper and broader than any other on this earth. You are called to that hope. There is a richness in fellowship with a family, who are each individually called to holiness, the family of God. Being surrounded by this family, you will continue to be blessed by this inheritance from God. You have also been given great power in Christ, to be victorious in your own life and to bless others.

> "I pray also that the eyes of your heart may be enlightened in order that you may know the hope to which He has called you, the riches of His glorious inheritance in the saints, and His incomparably great power for us who believe." **Ephesians 1:18,19a**

**Write how these truths bless your life.**

________________________________________

________________________________________

________________________________________

________________________________________

________________________________________

________________________________________

________________________________________

________________________________________

________________________________________

________________________________________

285. By the grace of the Lord's forgiveness, you are blameless. Your life is clean, innocent and pure in Christ Jesus. You have a strength deep inside, because you have been healed of a huge hurt. The process of healing has developed this strength, which was previously unknown. It is a strength that is wrapped in the faithfulness of God. Your life is in Him now, not in the sad memory of the past. He will continue to empower your life with His own virtues. You will never again be burdened with past pain, but will be able to claim victory over your former weaknesses.

> "He will keep you strong to the end, so that you will be blameless on the day of our Lord Jesus Christ. God, who has called you into fellowship with His Son Jesus Christ our Lord, is faithful." **1 Corinthians 1:8,9**

**Write about the faithfulness of God in your life.**

______________________________________________

______________________________________________

______________________________________________

______________________________________________

______________________________________________

______________________________________________

______________________________________________

______________________________________________

______________________________________________

______________________________________________

286. Your love for God has led you to follow His direction for your life. You have learned to receive His tremendous love, soaking in its warmth and tenderness. By affirming your identity in your Savior and Healer, Jesus, you are placing your entire life in the Lord's hands. He has a new promise of love and grace that will fulfill your life. It is a promise beyond comprehension. He has prepared for you new experiences, new fellowship in His family, as well as new opportunities to be blessed and to bless others. The only thing you need to do is rest in the Lord, trusting Him with all your heart and soul.

> "No eye has seen, no ear has heard, no mind has conceived what God has prepared for those who love Him."
>
> **1 Corinthians 2:9b**

**Write about trusting God for His promises.**

287. Since the Spirit of God is in you, your healing from the trauma of your past is complete and victorious. You have overcome Satan's attempt to keep you from the grace of Christ. Even though there may be physical consequences from the trauma that you still live with, the grace of Christ enables you to do so with a peace in your soul. The victory is yours in Christ Jesus. His Spirit is with you every day. The power of God exceeds every evil thing Satan would try to toss at you.

> "You, dear children, are from God and have overcome them, because the One who is in you is greater than the one who is in the world." **1 John 4:4**

**Write about being an overcomer by the power of God's Spirit in you.**

___

___

___

___

___

___

___

___

___

___

288. You may have tried to deal with the pain of your past by overworking, overeating, medicating with alcohol or drugs, or meditation. None of these attempts would reach the root of the problem. Without the Spirit of God present in the process, nothing will heal the damaged soul. True healing, the kind that seeps down into your soul, is only possible by the grace of Christ Jesus working in your life through the Holy Spirit. It is not your might that helps you step away from feeling like a victim the rest of your life. It is the Spirit of God who gives you the miracle of a new identity, a self image of the victorious person God created you to be. This transformation is only made by divine power, not any human power of suggestion or action.

> "'Not by might nor by power, but by my Spirit,' says the Lord Almighty." **Zechariah 4:6b**

**Write about the Holy Spirit and His work in your life.**

________________________________________

________________________________________

________________________________________

________________________________________

________________________________________

________________________________________

________________________________________

________________________________________

________________________________________

289. You have a new inheritance in Christ. It has started with a new concept of self. As you live in the victorious identity which He has given you, new gifts from God will emerge. There may be new friendships that bless your soul and new opportunities you had never imagined. His inheritance for you is eternal, but it starts now. It is fullness of life, abundance in Christ. The ultimate joy in this inheritance is that you are able to experience your relationship with God as Daddy God and be His beloved son or daughter.

> "He who overcomes will inherit all this, and I will be his God and he will be my son." **Revelation 21:7**

**Write about your inheritance from God.**

___

___

___

___

___

___

___

___

___

___

___

290. Take a moment to read the passage from today. It is a most beautiful description of your identity in Christ. The attributes of Christ, the Father God, and the Holy Spirit are displayed in beauty through the words of the psalmist. Love and faithfulness have met together in your life. The kiss of divine righteousness and peace has healed your soul. You are fulfilled in the faithfulness of a Holy God.

> "Love and faithfulness meet together; righteousness and peace kiss each other. Faithfulness springs forth from the earth, and righteousness looks down from heaven."
>
> **Psalm 85:10,11**

**Write how this scripture blesses you.**

291. You have been raised up out of terrible suffering and seated with Christ in the heavenly realms. How is this possible? Your spirit is the place where God connects with you. There is an aspect of your spirit that is connected with your body, still on Earth—in the physical realm. Part of your spirit is already connecting with God in the heavenly realms, by the power of the Holy Spirit working in you. You will never need to go back to the victim mentality, which was stuck in the mire of the physical. Your spirit has been freed and you are victorious in Christ!

> "And God raised us up with Christ and seated us with Him in the heavenly realms in Christ Jesus." **Ephesians 2:6**

**Write about being seated with Christ in the heavenly realms.**

292. There is now a dramatic difference in how you perceive life. God's healing power has filled your life with light and beauty. You are open to the glory of God being displayed in the world. Your emotions have been freed from the jumble of past pains. Praise will become as natural as breathing, as you grow in your new-found identity-a truly victorious child of the King, Make a conscious effort to develop a joyful heart and a life of praise.

> "Through Jesus, therefore, let us continually offer to God a sacrifice of praise—the fruit of lips that confess His Name." **Hebrews 13:15**

**Write the praises of your heart.**

293. The Spirit of God has been leading you through the healing process. It is His Word and His glory that has enabled you to take courageous steps to set aside victimization, to embrace your self-image in Christ. Now, He is leading you in triumph, with other believers, in a procession of faith. Your life is and will continue to be a witness for God's glory. Through you, people will be drawn to the wonderful fragrance of knowing the grace of the Lord Jesus. The way this is accomplished in your life is through an exciting new journey of discovering the gifts God has placed in you, to be used for His glory.

> "But thanks be to God, who always leads us in triumphal procession in Christ and through us spreads everywhere the fragrance of the knowledge of Him."
>
> **2 Corinthians 2:14**

**Write about completing your journey of healing and beginning this new journey of grace.**

__________________________________________________

__________________________________________________

__________________________________________________

__________________________________________________

__________________________________________________

__________________________________________________

__________________________________________________

__________________________________________________

__________________________________________________

294. Remember to lift up your soul to the Lord. Every day, take time to reconnect your spirit with the Spirit of God. As you balance family, work and personal time, do everything with the guiding tenderness of the Holy Spirit. Your life is defined by the grace of God, making it easy to be a servant of grace. The Lord's love covers you, so that His joy will flow through you to others.

> "Bring joy to your servant, for to you, O Lord, I lift up my soul." **Psalm 86:4**

**Write about the joy the Lord has brought to your life.**

295. One of the many confirmations of your healing is freedom to worship the Lord. Before this, your arms and hands may have felt like lead weights, making your heart so burdened that you weren't able to truly enter into worship. As you laid aside your victim mentality and placed your identity in Christ Jesus, worship began to come alive in your spirit and in your body, too. Allow yourself to worship freely, with your arms and hands lifted high to the Lord and your voice singing His praises.

> "Lift up your hands in the sanctuary and praise the Lord." **Psalm 134:2**

**Write how worship has changed for you. Take a moment to thank God for those changes and praise Him for His holiness and grace.**

___

___

___

___

___

___

___

___

___

___

___

296. Think for a moment about the songs of a bruised heart that you used to sing. Perhaps lyrics like, "Oh, I am so broken and sad," came from your heart and out of your mouth with less than a melody. The songs of your heart are quite different now. They may be more like the wonderful hymns of the church, such as, "Be Thou My Vision, My One True God." Perhaps you sing contemporary praise songs, such as, "Open The Eyes of My Heart Lord, I Want To See You." It is the right thing for you to do, to sing joyfully of the Lord and His grace.

> "Sing joyfully to the Lord, you righteous; it is fitting for the upright to praise Him." **Psalm 33:1**

**Write about the song of your heart and your joy in singing to the Lord.**

________________________________________

________________________________________

________________________________________

________________________________________

________________________________________

________________________________________

________________________________________

________________________________________

________________________________________

________________________________________

297. Into every area of your life, Christ has brought healing. Even your sleep may have been affected by your suffering. You may be experiencing for the first time what a truly peaceful sleep is like, and how it feels to fall asleep knowing you are loved. God's love for you is intensely more profound than any other; His peace sinks down into your soul. Allow yourself to receive this great joy from God. Become more aware each day of His love and your joy in receiving it.

> "I will lie down and sleep in peace, for you alone, O Lord, make me dwell in safety." **Psalm 4:8**

**Write about sleeping in peace, being completely in the will of God and being held in His love.**

___

___

___

___

___

___

___

___

___

___

___

298. The Lord has healed your heart and your spirit, to the point where you are prepared for the challenges that come each day. Give thanks to God for both the positive and the negative, for in each are lessons of grace. Christ Jesus has power over negative things, using them to make a positive impact in your life. This is real living, vital and exciting in Christ. Enjoy music as a part of your day, every day lifting your praises to God.

> "Sing and make music in your heart to the Lord, always giving thanks to God the Father for everything, in the Name of our Lord Jesus Christ." **Ephesians 5:19b,20**

**Write how music blesses you and helps you to focus on God.**

299. The Lord is doing a mighty work in your life; by His power and grace you are being progressively healed. You are just beginning to experience His greatness. Keep your heart in tune with His Spirit; He will surprise you with more blessings. God's blessings of grace and empowerment may come through relationships, increased abilities, or insight and wisdom. Continue in praise to God for every act of His power.

> "Praise Him for His acts of power; praise Him for His surpassing greatness." **Psalm 150:2**

**List a few of His mighty acts of power in your life.**
**Take a moment to praise Him and thank Him.**

___________________________________________

___________________________________________

___________________________________________

___________________________________________

___________________________________________

___________________________________________

___________________________________________

___________________________________________

___________________________________________

___________________________________________

___________________________________________

300. You have been blessed by Father God in a way no earthly father could match. The spiritual blessings that come through Jesus, lift you beyond a mere earthly existence into the heavenly realms. There is no need to indulge in sadness, self-pity, or to overfill your days with activity. It may still be a challenge to focus on the Lord and His gift of spiritual blessings to you. He will bring to you people and situations that will best help you grow, increasingly revealing to you the destiny for which you were specifically formed.

> "Praise be to the God and Father of our Lord Jesus Christ, who has blessed us in the heavenly realms with every spiritual blessing in Christ." **Ephesians 1:3**

**Learn to wait on the Lord to reveal, each new day, what He has for your life. Write about how He has blessed you in these ways.**

301. You have a vibrant, growing relationship with the awesome Triune God. As a result, you will one day experience fully His splendor and majesty. Your continued strength and joy have their source in Him. Develop a sense of wonder, of awe, before your God. His grace has changed your life so dramatically. You have a new life of joy in Him.

> "Splendor and majesty are before Him; strength and joy in His dwelling place." **1 Chronicles 16:27**

**Describe how awareness of the Lord's majesty has enriched your life.**

302. May God's grace pour over your spirit. You may not have even understood what the wounding did to your soul and spirit, but God knew. His grace was with you, sustaining you until the time was right for true healing in Him. You have had courage and determination to follow His leading, even when it was difficult. His grace covered you every step of the way. Your love for the Lord is growing deeper as you grow in Him. His love for you is eternal and ever flowing. May the grace of the Father, the Son, and the Spirit be your source for all of life's needs.

> "Grace to all who love our Lord Jesus Christ with an undying love." **Ephesians 6:24**

**Write about your love of the Lord Jesus and His grace in your spirit.**

303. Jesus is able to keep you from falling back into feeling like a victim. In Him, you are clean and pure and without fault. In grace, He presents you to the Father, filled with joy and love. He has chosen you and given His love, that you would experience healing and eternal life in Him. Give Him the glory today and every day.

> "To Him who is able to keep you from falling and to present you before His glorious Presence without fault and with great joy—to the only God, our Savior be glory, majesty, power and authority, through Jesus Christ our Lord, before all ages, now and forever. Amen."
>
> **Jude 24,25**

**Write about the aspect of these verses that really bless your soul.**

___________________________________________

___________________________________________

___________________________________________

___________________________________________

___________________________________________

___________________________________________

___________________________________________

___________________________________________

___________________________________________

___________________________________________

___________________________________________

304. Hold onto the strength and power of the Lord God. Your suffering was real, but it no longer has the power to hold you captive. Your new life is in Christ, in His love and power. You will be able to do wonderful things in the awesome Name of Jesus Christ. You will bless many people through the unique qualities and abilities Christ has blessed you with. Be strong as He teaches you. Walk in His power and know that you are His beloved.

"Finally, be strong in the Lord and in His mighty power."

**Ephesians 6:10**

**Write just a bit of what His strength and power means to you.**

# Chapter 6: Beyond Pain, Reaching Out to Others

In this chapter, consider the totality of a fire; its beauty reflects the majesty, love, and passion of the Triune God. Your life also resembles a fire, as a witness to the glory of God. Fan the flame of God's love and His unique gifting in your life. Explore the concept of giving others the warmth of this healing love that is in Christ.

305. Jesus is guiding your mind and your spirit through healing and into His righteousness. He has restored your soul from the horrendous pain you suffered. You are in His path of righteousness. The final step to complete your healing is to reach out to other people with the love that has so blessed your life. To hold this blessing of healing only to yourself would mean stagnation and eventually self focus once again. Keeping your spirit in tune with the Lord will move you into His perfect will to bless others.

> "He restores my soul. He guides me in the paths of righteousness for His Name's sake." **Psalm 23:3**

**Write your thoughts about walking in this new path of righteousness, for the glory of His Name.**

___

___

___

___

___

___

___

___

___

___

___

306. Trust the Lord to lift you up. Embrace a tender humility before Him; His work in you will shine forth and show His grace. You are righteous in Christ and are deeply loved! Wait on the Lord, watching for confirmation, the opening or closing of doors in divine direction. Then step out in confidence of His grace; the Lord God will bless you as He lifts you up. You will be blessed greatly as He confirms to you that you are doing just as He desires.

> "The Lord lifts up those who are bowed down, the Lord loves the righteous." **Psalm 146:8b**

**Write how you feel in genuine humility before the Lord, in anticipation of a new mighty work in you by His grace.**

307. The Lord's love is so good; it enfolds you in comfort and peace. The faithfulness of His Word is eternal for those who will receive it. The power and grace of the Lord Jesus is available for every generation. Now that you have received extensively of the Lord's faithfulness and love, reach out beyond yourself to share it in any way possible. You have received a great healing; share the wonderful love that the Lord has brought into your life.

"The Lord is good and His love endures forever; His faithfulness continues through all generations." **Psalm 100:5**

**Write about becoming a part of God's eternal faithfulness by sharing His love.**

308. As you are willing to share the wonderful news of what the Lord has done for you, trust Him completely for divine direction. The Holy Spirit will guide you with gentle promptings. Be sensitive to His affirmation. In everything you do, confirm the Lord's Presence in your life. The Lord will bring to your heart, mind and spirit, the exact way in which He wants you to bless His loved ones. His timing is also perfect. Begin to watch for the opportunities He brings into your life and the awesome timing for blessing others.

> "Trust in the Lord with all your heart and lean not on your own understanding; in all your ways acknowledge Him, and He will make your paths straight." **Proverbs 3:5,6**

**Write about trusting the Lord to make your path straight.**

309. These verses have been the inspiration for this book. God has given you a unique gift! By going through all the steps of healing, you are fanning into flame the gift that He placed in you. You were once so full of pain that you were either afraid, angry, or aggressive on the outside, yet timid in your spirit. God has removed the timidity to reveal what He has placed in you, His Spirit of power, of love, and of self-control. It is by the power of the Holy Spirit working in your life that the gift is growing into a fire of glory to honor the Almighty God.

> "For this reason I remind you to fan into flame the gift of God, which is in you through the laying on of my hands. For God did not give us a spirit of timidity, but a Spirit of power, of love, and of self-discipline."
>
> **2 Timothy 1:6,7**

**Acknowledge in writing that God has placed a gift in your soul and it is being fanned into a flame for His glory.**

310. You are unique in all the universe because God chose you and has loved you from before creation. His grace has sustained you through suffering and has blessed you with the healing of deep wounds. The Lord has also consecrated you for His purpose of blessing others with His love. Underlying your divinely given gift is a strength born out of adversity. You have an empathy filled with personal knowledge of suffering. Ask the Lord Jesus to clarify your particular gift in His grace.

> "We have different gifts, according to the grace given us."
>
> **Romans 12:6**

**Write a prayer seeking His wisdom about your gift and how He would have you use it.**

311. Stretch out in faith to use the gift that God has placed within you. Recognize the wonderful truth of God's grace, that you have been given this gift to serve others. When you do so, you are being faithful to God's call upon your life. The Lord Jesus was faithful in the giving of His life. As a result, you have forgiveness and eternal, abundant life. Your gift is important to those who would come to know the fullness of love in divine grace through you. Be willing to administer God's grace with the depth of feeling that He has blessed you with.

> "Each one should use whatever gift he has received to serve others, faithfully administering God's grace in its various forms." **1 Peter 4:10**

**Write a prayer of commitment to use your gift to serve others in the love and grace of Christ.**

312. Whether a gift of teaching, encouragement, hospitality, or a myriad of others, your gift is to help bring people to Christ and to build them up in Christian maturity. This is to prepare God's people for their own works of service. You are an example, of a life that has been changed by the grace of God and the power of His glory. Be willing to share what the Lord has done in your life. Be sensitive to the individuals the Lord brings into your life; seek His wisdom to be loving and gracious. It is such an honor to be a blessing to another in Christ!

> "To prepare God's people for works of service, so that the body of Christ may be built up." **Ephesians 4:12**

**Write how you feel that God has called you to help build up His people.**

313. The Lord has given you peace, healing the hurts of your past, to bless your life in His grace. Bring His peace to others, encouraging true peace in His grace and love. By example, you are able to show others that true peace is attained first by facing difficult issues with Christ. He gives the strength needed to work through them. Secondly, true peace comes by dealing with all the facets of those issues with the truth of the Word of God. Finally, place your entire life in Christ and His grace. Be a peacemaker and receive the blessing of God.

> "Blessed are the peacemakers, for they will be called the sons of God." **Matthew 5:9**

**Write about your desire to be a peacemaker for the Lord.**

314. With the healing from your past, the qualities that the Lord has built into your spirit are more fully emerging. Gentleness is much more a part of your life, because the hurt you experienced has been given the salve of grace in Christ Jesus. Allow that gentleness to radiate God's love to your family, friends and acquaintances. The Lord is near you, every moment guiding you by His Spirit. People will see His grace working through your life.

"Let your gentleness be evident to all. The Lord is near."
**Philippians 4:5**

**Write about having gentleness in your life as a testimony of the Lord's grace.**

315. The Lord has given you in His Word, all of the tools that you need to grow in faith. The verse for today is a wonderful example of this. Embrace the wisdom of the Word of God. Hold onto the love and faithfulness of the Lord with all your heart. Allow the Lord Jesus to fill you with His love and faithfulness. His grace has changed your life and will fulfill you through and through.

> "Let love and faithfulness never leave you; bind them around your neck, write them on the tablet of your heart." **Proverbs 3:3**

**Write about love and faithfulness in your life.**

316. When you choose to have empathy for another person for the suffering they are enduring or have endured, you are lifting his, or her burden to the throne of God. Your own suffering and healing now becomes a fulcrum of strength to help another person. Through your gentle encouragement, the Lord will bless those who suffer. The marvelous miracle of this is that as you reach out in genuine compassion, your own healing will come to a new level. You are enabled to reach out with the compassion of Christ.

> "Carry each other's burdens, and in this way you will fulfill the law of Christ." **Galatians 6:2**

**Write how the Lord has given you empathy for those who suffer.**

317. As you stretch forth to help others, there may be times when the Lord gently corrects you. He wants you to be firmly in His will. Sometimes it is easy to get sidetracked by what seems good and right. Trust in the Lord and His love for you. His discipline is for you to grow in faith and in power, to accomplish what He would have you do. Try to learn carefully the lesson from the Lord. You are maturing in Christ. You are no longer a victim, but are now a strong witness for the glory of Christ. If you find yourself feeling really bad, ask the Lord in prayer to remove the negative response that was so much a part of your suffering, replacing it with understanding and a feeling of being loved.

> "Blessed is the man whom God corrects; so do not despise the discipline of the Almighty." **Job 5:17**

**Write how you feel when the Lord corrects you.**

_______________

_______________

_______________

_______________

_______________

_______________

_______________

_______________

_______________

_______________

318. It is really important for you to be able to discern the difference of the Lord's discipline from any abusive experience of human correction. The Lord loves you and wants you to be blessed and mature in Him. His correction serves to make you stronger in Him. It may be as simple as softening your spirit when you are helping others. It may be a bit stinging, such as revealing to you a judgmental attitude. When you learn from His gentle correction, your efforts will continue to be filled with His grace. What a wonderful promise, that you will produce a harvest of righteousness and peace!

> "No discipline seems pleasant at the time, but painful. Later on, however, it produces a harvest of righteousness and peace for those who have been trained by it."
>
> **Hebrews 12:11**

**Write about learning to receive correction from the Lord.**

319. God has helped you along the journey of healing from your past. You are now making a huge transition, from focusing on your pain and distress, to being available to God for His work of grace through you to others. When you feel overwhelmed or confused, seek the wisdom and counsel of the Lord. He will support you and guide you in every situation. Be willing to listen, for His Spirit will speak His wisdom to your mind and confirm it in your spirit.

> "To God belong wisdom and power; counsel and understanding are His." **Job 12:13**

**Write about seeking the Lord's wisdom as you learn to share His grace.**

320. Continue to develop your prayer time with the Lord. It is your personal, intimate connection with your Lord. Come to Him with every request, no matter how small or seemingly inconsequential. Every aspect of your life is more important to the Lord of grace than you may ever realize. His love and understanding has no boundaries. Take time to explore prayer, conversational prayer with others, and personal prayer with just you and the Lord. Prayer is a journey with the Lord that will continue from this moment throughout eternity.

> "And pray in the Spirit on all occasions with all kinds of prayers and requests. With this in mind, be alert and always keep on praying for all the saints." **Ephesians 6:18**

**Write something about prayer, your desires, your needs, or how your relationship with God has deepened through prayer.**

321. When you begin to talk to others about God and how He has blessed you with healing, God is maturing you in His grace. When you share the miracles of your own life, you are able to speak from personal experience with enthusiasm. Think about the difference from the years of pain and suffering to being fulfilled with the Lord's love. You have a remarkable story to share! God has equipped you to be able to share it in a unique way that will bless many people.

> "I will praise you, O Lord, with all my heart; I will tell of all your wonders." **Psalm 9:1**

**Write about sharing your experience with the Lord.**

322. As you share your story of healing, you will also be helping other people to open their hearts and lives to His healing grace. They may be closed to any opportunity to receive the Lord, yet receptive to your sharing. The Lord stands next to those who are hurting, but sometimes they don't even realize it. You are a voice of hope, bringing the grace of the Lord Jesus Christ to people who are stuck in their pain.

> "With my mouth I will greatly extol the Lord; in the great throng I will praise Him. For He stands at the right hand of the needy one, to save his life from those who condemn him." **Psalm 109:30,31**

**Write about being a voice of hope, of the grace that is in Christ.**

323. A difficult lesson in the process of maturing in Christ is to fully accept others without pre-judging them. God has formed you like a beautiful green tree. You can choose to look critically at the other seedlings around you, thinking how immature and imperfect they are; or you can lift your branches skyward in praise, fully in acceptance of all the plants of the earth as each struggles to find his way upward to the light of God. As you mature in Christ, you may see others who seem to be not on the "right" path. Pray for them, seeking God's wisdom to share in His perfect grace.

> "Accept one another, then, just as Christ accepted you, in order to bring praise to God." **Romans 15:7**

**Write about accepting others as Christ loves and accepts you.**

324. Another aspect of maturing in Christ is the ability to recognize and deal with sin appropriately in your life. While still on earth, you have the propensity to sin, but do not have to be a slave to it. Develop trusted Christian friends who can help you be accountable to God, both in your words and actions. Pray for each other; it is a gift of grace to be cleansed by the Lord and have such intimate fellowship and trust. Continue your prayer, on behalf of those you know who are hurting and in need of grace. You are righteous before God; your prayers are powerful and effective.

> "Therefore confess your sins to each other and pray for each other so that you may be healed. The prayer of a righteous man is powerful and effective." **James 5:16**

**Write about confession and prayer and the name of at least one trusted friend with whom you can pray.**

______________________________________________

______________________________________________

______________________________________________

______________________________________________

______________________________________________

______________________________________________

______________________________________________

______________________________________________

______________________________________________

______________________________________________

325. God is doing a marvelous work of grace in your life. He is equipping you with everything good for the work He has called you to. The process began with healing and now is taking you beyond what you had ever thought possible to do work that is pleasing to God. Learn the things that God is teaching you each day. Fill yourself up with His Word. Continue to seek Him and His perfect timing for learning and sharing His grace.

> "May the God of peace, who through the blood of the eternal covenant brought back from the dead our Lord Jesus, that great Shepherd of the sheep, equip you with everything good for doing His will, and may He work in us what is pleasing to Him, through Jesus Christ, to whom be glory for ever and ever. Amen."
>
> **Hebrews 13:20,21**

**Write about being equipped in the Lord.**

326. In the process of being equipped for ministry, learning to obey those who are in authority over you is essential. God places individuals in authority over you for specific reasons. The first is accountability. You are responsible to use your time and resources wisely. God knows your heart and your actions; you are instantly accountable to God. The second reason is respect. If you learn to respect the leadership over you, the work will be a joy for you and for those in authority. Learning respect for authority also deepens your respect for God. His work in you brings joy to your heart.

> "Obey your leaders and submit to their authority. They keep watch over you as men who must give an account. Obey them so their work will be a joy, not a burden, for that would be of no advantage to you." **Hebrews 13:17**

**Write about learning to submit to authority and trusting God to be your ultimate authority.**

______________________________________________

______________________________________________

______________________________________________

______________________________________________

______________________________________________

______________________________________________

______________________________________________

______________________________________________

______________________________________________

327. A huge part of healing has been to learn a new self image in the grace of Christ. Your new awareness of yourself makes you comfortable with being chosen, loved and of inestimable value in the Lord. Yet, because of the process you have come through, your spirit is humble before the God of the universe. This humility is a foundation stone of your life in ministry. As God blesses other people through your efforts, they will share their gratitude and even praise the gifts you have. Give God the glory and praise for the great work He is doing in you. The Lord has lifted you out of a pit of despair for His gracious purpose. Avoid pride as if it were a poison jellyfish.

> "'Let him who boasts, boast in the Lord,' For it is not the one who commends himself who is approved, but the one whom the Lord commends." **2 Corinthians 10:17b,18**

**Boast of the Lord, all over the page, with big writing, colorful and decorated!**

328. Jesus has given you a great commission. You have received so much from the Holy God! Now it is time to share it, that others may come to receive Christ too, and be healed. It is more than just an introduction to Christ. He calls you to relationship building, helping others to receive Him and then grow in Him. The way in which you do this will involve the unique gift that the Lord has given you. The wonderful part of all this is that the Spirit of the Lord is always with you, guiding you and supporting you.

> "Then Jesus came to them and said, 'All authority in Heaven and on Earth has been given to me. Therefore go and make disciples of all nations, baptizing them in the Name of the Father and of the Son and of the Holy Spirit, and teaching them to obey everything I have commanded you. And surely I am with you always, to the very end of the age.' " **Matthew 28:18–20**

**Write about how the great commission applies to your life.**

____________________________________________

____________________________________________

____________________________________________

____________________________________________

____________________________________________

____________________________________________

____________________________________________

____________________________________________

____________________________________________

329. It is so awesome to realize you are a part of the divine plan of redemption. God has called you to be a voice as a witness to His mighty power and boundless love. Your willingness to be that voice for Christ confirms His continuing work of grace in your life. It is the grace of Christ that will open the eyes and hearts of people to the Lord. He will bring them out of darkness to light, from the power of Satan to God. You will share in the great joy of blessings as they unfold in the lives of people you minister to.

> "I am sending you to them to open their eyes and turn them from darkness to light, and from the power of Satan to God, so that they may receive forgiveness of sins and a place among those who are sanctified by faith in me." **Acts 26:17b,18**

**Write of your desire to bring others to Christ, who heals so powerfully.**

____________________________________________________________

____________________________________________________________

____________________________________________________________

____________________________________________________________

____________________________________________________________

____________________________________________________________

____________________________________________________________

____________________________________________________________

____________________________________________________________

330. Jesus honors your willing obedience to be His witness before men and women, boys and girls. He promises to bring your name to Father God, perhaps even sharing an intimate moment of joy with Him of your commitment to all that is holy. When you share with others, from your own experience, what the power of the Lord can do, and how much He loves His children, grace flows. The Father, the Son, and the Holy Spirit will fill the atmosphere with spiritual power for salvation.

> "Whoever acknowledges me before men, I will also acknowledge him before my Father in Heaven."
>
> **Matthew 10:32**

**Write how you are beginning to share God's love and what He has done for you.**

331. Your days may begin to be filled with tiny steps of service for others. Whether at a job, with many tasks to be done, or with little children, with unending needs, do each thing in the Name of Jesus and His love. When finishing that report or mending those ripped trousers, let your attitude shift from, "Must I?" to "It is a joy to do this as unto the Lord." Let God develop within you the loving heart of His true servant. Find a reason to thank God for the task and what you learn through it or how it will enable you to share His love with another. When opportunities arise that are appropriate for sharing the fullness of the Gospel and your story of healing, share and rejoice!

> "And whatever you do, whether in word or deed, do it all in the Name of the Lord Jesus, giving thanks to God the Father through Him." **Colossians 3:17**

**Write about bringing Christ into your everyday tasks.**

________________________________________

________________________________________

________________________________________

________________________________________

________________________________________

________________________________________

________________________________________

________________________________________

________________________________________

332. It is delightful to realize that God is the Lord of the harvest. It is His work in the hearts of hurting people that brings about the harvest of salvation. It is an honor to participate as a worker in such a harvest! As you are stretching forth to be a worker in God's great harvest, pray that God would lift up many to work with you. You will have new opportunities for fellowship in the body of Christ as you open yourself to ministry. There will be many blessings as you join in the harvest.

> "Then He said to His disciples, 'The harvest is plentiful but the workers are few. Ask the Lord of the harvest, therefore, to send out workers into His harvest field.'"
> **Matthew 9:37,38**

**Write how God is encouraging you to be a worker in His harvest field.**

333. The Lord has supplied all your need. His tremendous love fulfills your deepest need. His grace has been there, helping you to survive the years of suffering and go through the steps of healing. Further, God promises to enlarge the harvest of your righteousness. Take time to ponder how wonderful this promise is. When you follow the direction of the Holy Spirit into ministry, you are in the center of God's will. You will experience a great harvest that grows out of your righteousness in Christ. The blessing of this harvest is that God's grace ripples as drops of water, blessing those you may not know with the fruit of your ministry.

> "Now He who supplies seed to the sower and bread for food will also supply and increase your store of seed and will enlarge the harvest of your righteousness."
>
> **2 Corinthians 9:10**

**Write how this promise makes you feel.**

334. Bring the warmth of God's love into your everyday life. Take time for loved ones and friends, and those with whom you come in contact. Give of your time and of the love that God has placed in you. Sometimes it may be physical, such as caring for someone after a surgery. Or it may be listening a couple of hours a week for six months or so, in a long-term friendship. Being a friend in the grace of the Lord Jesus Christ is often a personal sacrifice on behalf of others. It is love, divinely filled with grace, which inspires such giving.

> "And do not forget to do good and to share with others, for with such sacrifices God is pleased." **Hebrews 13:16**

**Write about doing good for Christ.**

335. May the favor of the Lord rest upon you. His favor incorporates all His attributes in a divine grace that is incomparable. It is this favor that rests upon you. It is truly beyond understanding. Try to perceive the magnitude of the Lord's favor and receive it. Rejoice in it! It is God who establishes the work of grace He has for you. He prepares the way. He will bless you as you trust Him and step out in faith to do His work.

> "May the favor of the Lord our God rest upon us;
> establish the work of our hands for us — yes, establish
> the work of our hands." **Psalm 90:17**

**Write about the favor of God upon you and your work for Him.**

336. You have good news of God's love to bring to individuals who are weary of suffering. As you choose to do so, the grace of the Lord Jesus will bless your efforts. You will be so much more beautiful because of the beauty of that love shining through you. Christ brings a radiance to the face and a joy to the soul of one who shares His love with those who hurt. It is more than outward beauty. There is a deep elegance of commitment, faith, and truth in you. You have come through horrendous pain to a powerful, grace-filled healing and are now sharing that divine love.

> "How beautiful are the feet of those who bring good news!" **Romans 10:15b**

**Write about the beauty, inside and out, that Christ has brought to your life.**

337. Jesus has indeed given you a new song of joy! Think about the song of praise He has given you, a song of deliverance and healing. Prepare your heart to bring your song of joy to many people. God will bring them to you, either one by one, or many at the same time. They will respond to the truth of God in your testimony. This may be a new step in your spiritual walk, being a leader, a mentor, an encourager.

> "He put a new song in my mouth, a hymn of praise to our God. Many will see and fear and put their trust in the Lord." **Psalm 40:3**

**Write about your new song of praise; seek God's wisdom in prayer to prepare you to be a leader in His grace.**

338. As you reach out to others with the love of Christ, be very careful about the words you use. It is easy to gossip or joke at another's expense. Sometimes even tempers can flare and awful words can be exchanged. The uncontrolled tongue can be extremely hurtful. Work hard to keep all your words uplifting. When conflicts arise, deal with them in a truthful and gracious manner, respecting the opinions of others while upholding your own to be of value, too. Be open to viewing life from the perspective of those with whom you are interacting. Live your life full of grace, with words of encouragement and genuine love.

> "The tongue that brings healing is a tree of life, but a deceitful tongue crushes the spirit." **Proverbs 15:4**

**Write about the positive and negative aspects of words and how much they can hurt or heal.**

339. Think about your testimony of the Lord's grace in your life. Even write it down, to solidify in your mind and heart how much the Lord has done, covering the details of your salvation and healing. The reason to do so is preparation. You have a hope deep within your soul; be prepared to share the reason for that hope. Ministry often takes preparation and understanding, along with the grace of God supplying the miraculous way He reaches human hearts. God will bring many people to you, so be ready to respond to their questions of how your life is so blessed.

> "But in your hearts set apart Christ as Lord. Always be prepared to give an answer to everyone who asks you to give the reason for the hope that you have." **1 Peter 3:15a,b**

**Write a brief testimony of your story of suffering, and healing in Christ.**

________________________________________________

________________________________________________

________________________________________________

________________________________________________

________________________________________________

________________________________________________

________________________________________________

________________________________________________

________________________________________________

________________________________________________

340. The Spirit of the Lord is with you! He has anointed you to proclaim His love and grace. Christ quoted Isaiah 61:1–4 while announcing His divine mission. Christ Jesus is the One whom you are bringing people to. You are a voice for freedom in Christ to those who are oppressed by suffering. The Lord's favor is upon all who receive it; you have the honor to share it with those who don't even know. Rest for a moment, in the Lord's Presence, receiving this divine anointing. Ponder what the Holy Spirit is saying to your spirit.

> "The Spirit of the Lord is on me, because He has anointed me to preach good news to the poor. He has sent me to proclaim freedom for the prisoners and recovery of sight for the blind, to release the oppressed, to proclaim the year of the Lord's favor." **Luke 4:18,19**

**Write the words of the Holy Spirit to you, words of encouragement or direction.**

341. As you endeavor to share the Lord's love with others, your efforts will bear fruit. You are not only receiving his grace, but are actively living a life of righteousness. The life of righteousness becomes a tree of righteousness to many people. They pick the fruits of it — kindness, understanding, love, joy, peace — and their lives are changed. In coming close to you, they have come close to God as well. Their changed lives in Christ are the fruit of your righteous life. God will give you wisdom because of your willingness to reach out to others with the Gospel with your own story of healing.

> "The fruit of the righteous is a tree of life, and he who wins souls is wise." **Proverbs 11:30**

**Write about being righteous in Christ.**

342. As you develop in spiritual maturity, spiritual warfare will become a part of your work for the Lord. Satan will do anything to keep people away from the Lord, or to keep hurting Christians stuck in their pain. Demonic forces keep people immobile through manipulation of fear, pain and other emotional and spiritual factors. In Christ, you have power to demolish strongholds. Reach out with the divine strength of the Word of God. Share with others the hope that is in Christ and the power of His Word.

> "The weapons we fight with are not the weapons of the world. On the contrary, they have divine power to demolish strongholds. We demolish arguments and every pretension that sets itself up against the knowledge of God, and we make captive every thought to make it obedient to Christ." **2 Corinthians 10:4,5**

**Write how your life has been transformed by the power of God.**

343. You have chosen to follow Christ, who is the light of the world. He has brought healing to your soul. He has called you to a higher purpose than you have ever imagined. All the stuff Satan threw at you could not succeed because the Lord covered you with love and grace. The same is true for other people who receive Jesus Christ into their hearts and lives. Nothing can succeed against the Lord God. This truth gives you a confidence in ministry; Christ is a strong, sure foundation for hope.

> "There is no wisdom, no insight, no plan that can succeed against the Lord." **Proverbs 21:30**

**Write about your confidence in the power of God to bless His people.**

344. You have experienced how being immersed in the Word of God brings healing, wisdom, and truth into your life. Use the Word as you reach out to bless others. It is God's Word of comfort to a hurting world. The Holy Spirit blesses the Word of God to gently impress divine truth into many hearts and minds. Continue to study the Scriptures, to strengthen your walk with the Lord and to be thoroughly equipped for the good work of blessing God is leading you into.

> "All Scripture is God-breathed and is useful for teaching, rebuking, correcting and training in righteousness, so that the man of God may be thoroughly equipped for every good work." **2 Timothy 3:16,17**

**Write how God's Word has changed your life.**

345. You are able to stand firm in every situation because you have the truths of God in your life. In teaching about spiritual warfare, Paul speaks in terms of physical armament to describe the strength and power you have in Christ. Prepare to stand firm against Satan by putting on the belt of truth and the breastplate of righteousness. Have your feet ready to walk where God leads to carry the Gospel of peace to a world of unrest.

> "Stand firm then, with the belt of truth buckled around your waist, with the breastplate of righteousness in place, and with your feet fitted with the readiness that comes from the Gospel of peace." **Ephesians 6:14,15**

**Write about the spiritual armament that God has provided for you.**

______________________________________________

______________________________________________

______________________________________________

______________________________________________

______________________________________________

______________________________________________

______________________________________________

______________________________________________

______________________________________________

______________________________________________

346. Paul's words on spiritual warfare are so powerful; may the Lord God bless them as you apply them to your life. Use the shield of faith, your faith in the One True God, to extinguish those awful fiery arrows Satan throws at you. Faith in Christ is powerful, for He is full of power and glory. Your own salvation is secure, as a helmet strapped on is secure. The Word of God is the sword of the Spirit of God. It is an offensive weapon against Satan's attempts to attack God and His people.

> "In addition to all this, take up the shield of faith, with which you can extinguish all the flaming arrows of the evil one. Take the helmet of salvation and the sword of the Spirit, which is the Word of God."
>
> **Ephesians 6:16,17**

**Write how you have been empowered by the Word of God.**

________________________________________

________________________________________

________________________________________

________________________________________

________________________________________

________________________________________

________________________________________

________________________________________

________________________________________

________________________________________

347. Through His Word, God has been healing your wounds and equipping you for His glory to be revealed through you. Whatever gift He has placed in you, consider your primary focus to be an extension of the work of grace that Christ began. By the forgiveness of sins, Jesus provided the way of reconciliation to Father God. You have been given a specific gift that will help people to be reconciled to their Father God. What a wonderful joy it is to be a blessing to others in such a profound way!

> "All this is from God, who reconciled us to Himself through Christ and gave us the ministry of reconciliation; that God was reconciling the world to Himself in Christ, not counting men's sins against them. And He has committed to us the message of reconciliation."
>
> **2 Corinthians 5:18,19**

**Write about the ministry of reconciliation in your life.**

348. With this powerful verse, the final step of healing can fall into place. The Lord has given His divine comfort to you. You now have the opportunity to give that same comfort to others who are hurting. God has changed the most awful thing in your life to be a focal point for you to experience divine love and grace and share His comfort with others. This truth gives a new perspective of suffering. It is in the area of your worst pain that God so profoundly works His miracles, healing and ministry to bless you and others.

> "Praise be to the God and Father of our Lord Jesus Christ, the Father of compassion and the God of all comfort, who comforts us in all our troubles, so that we can comfort those in any trouble with the comfort we ourselves have received from God." **2 Corinthians 1:3,4**

**Write about comforting others with the comfort you have been given.**

________________________________________________________________________

________________________________________________________________________

________________________________________________________________________

________________________________________________________________________

________________________________________________________________________

________________________________________________________________________

________________________________________________________________________

________________________________________________________________________

________________________________________________________________________

349. The Lord brought you to Himself, perhaps through the influence of a loved one or friend. In the process of living a victorious life in Christ, you may have a similar opportunity to directly influence a person to seek the grace of Christ Jesus. It is God's work of grace in you that has eternal blessings. Seek the wisdom of the Holy Spirit in your spirit to fully understand the eternal consequences of your efforts as you share His grace with others.

> "Remember this: Whoever turns a sinner from the error of his way will save him from death and cover over a multitude of sins." **James 5:20**

**Write about the seriousness of the Lord's work in you, from a life of pain to healing, to reaching out with the eternal hope of grace.**

350. As you reach out to people with the love and grace of Jesus Christ, you are also giving your love to God. You are bringing honor to His Name. You will be blessed as you endeavor to bless others. He will bless your life with an excitement that is full of joy as you continue to share in your own unique way, your hope in the grace of Christ.

> "God is not unjust; He will not forget your work and the love you have shown Him as you have helped His people and continue to help them." **Hebrews 6:10**

**Write how receiving God's love and sharing it with others has changed your life.**

351. The Lord God will always be with you. He has saved you and quieted your heart with His profound love. He takes delight in you, His beloved. He rejoices over you with singing. His joy is in your healing; your life in Him is like a waterfall of love pouring over you. Be refreshed in His love for you. Be thankful for His Presence in each step of healing. Ask Him to touch you each day with grace as you reach out to others with His great love. Allow yourself to receive His love and rejoicing over you.

> "The Lord your God is with you. He is mighty to save. He will take great delight in you, He will quiet you with His love, He will rejoice over you with singing."
>
> **Zephaniah 3:17**

**Write how this love fills a need deep inside, for approval, for affection and for a Father's love.**

352. Your healing in Christ Jesus has brought a maturity into your life, a spiritual maturity that comes of leaning on the Word of God with your very life. There is an intensity that is borne out of suffering and is matured through the grace and love of Christ Jesus. Keep that intensity, using it to bless others. Allow the Word of God to become a part of your life, richly blessing your soul and spirit. His Word will continue to change your life, bringing even more healing to your spirit. This is a lifelong process of God revealing to you, in His Word, His majesty, power, tender love, and transforming grace for your life.

> "Let the Word of Christ dwell in you richly as you teach and admonish one another with all wisdom, and as you sing psalms, hymns, and spiritual songs with gratitude in your hearts to God." **Colossians 3:16**

**Write about your joy in the Word of God.**

353. You have accomplished so very much in such an intense season of healing. You are now reaching out to others who are in pain and in need of the grace and love of Jesus Christ. You are also an integral part of the body of Christ. You have a life story of great endurance, healing and encouragement in Christ. Join in unity with others, sharing the grace that Christ has blessed you with. Receive their gifts of love and grace, so that together you may honor and glorify God.

> "May the God who gives endurance and encouragement give you a spirit of unity among yourselves as you follow Christ Jesus, so that with one heart and mouth you may glorify the God and Father of our Lord Jesus Christ."
>
> **Romans 15:5,6**

**Write about the spirit of unity you are able to have with others in the body of Christ and how it feels to be in community.**

354. The Lord is leading you on a path of righteousness, for His glory to be revealed in you. This season of healing has been for you to truly experience God's full love for you as His dear child. You needed each step, each moment of soaking in the love of the Lord God. God has also been preparing you to step beyond the healing process into a life of joyous service for Him. You have just begun to see the gleam of the dawn upon this path He has prepared. As you walk in faith, the path will be more and more illuminated by the grace of His Presence in your life.

> "The path of the righteous is like the first gleam of dawn, shining ever brighter till the full light of day."
>
> **Proverbs 4:18**

**Write about trusting God and stepping out in His path of righteousness.**

355. Whatever direction the Lord guides you, follow Him completely, with your mind, body, and spirit committed to Him. In today's verse, God gives you another promise of His grace in your life. He will make your righteousness shine, for it has its foundation in His righteousness. The justice of your cause, the deepest desire you have for His justice to prevail, will also shine because of His favor on you. Because of your heart and your commitment to the Lord God, people will see the brightness of God's true justice.

> "Commit your ways to the Lord; trust in Him and He will do this: He will make your righteousness shine like the dawn, the justice of your cause like the noonday sun."
>
> **Psalm 37:5,6**

**Write how this promise blesses you.**

356. Do not allow yourself to fall into a pattern of remaining silent about what God has done for you. Explore new ways of sharing your joy. Your gift may be a musical ability or teaching children. You may be an encourager or one who opens your home in hospitality. Wait for the Lord's prompting, so that those with whom you share will be receptive. Allow your joy to be seen, heard and felt by other people, who may need hope in God just at the moment you are sharing.

> "That my heart may sing to you and not be silent, O Lord my God, I will give you thanks forever." **Psalm 30:12**

**Write about one new way of sharing your joy of what God has done in your life.**

357. Jesus confronted the hypocrisy of the Pharisees in this passage. They strictly kept the Mosaic laws for washing and cleansing the body, but did not deal with the uncleanness of the heart. You have gone through not only cleansing of sin through faith in Jesus Christ, but a thorough cleansing of the pain in your life through His healing process. This verse brings out another aspect of your continuing journey. Often, feeling devalued by abuse or trauma leads to the outward expression of that devaluation in not taking care of personal appearance or living areas. If this has been an area of difficulty for you, begin to restore your appearance and living area to reflect your healing in Christ. Give permission to yourself to be beautiful and to live in a beautiful home.

"'Blind Pharisee! First clean the inside of the cup and dish and then the outside also will be clean.'" **Matthew 23:26**

**Write about taking new steps of healing by cleaning and embracing beauty.**

___

___

___

___

___

___

___

___

___

358. Keep your heart and mind focused on the Lord. Seek Him and His grace for your life. Develop a routine of waiting on the Lord, for every aspect of your life. Listen to the Holy Spirit, for gentle direction to share the joy of your life in grace. Be ready to do so, with the same gentleness of the Spirit, trusting God to use your life for His glory. In worship, lift up God in exaltation, for He is the One who is worthy of all praise.

> "But may all who seek you rejoice and be glad in you; may those who love your salvation always say, 'Let God be exalted!'" **Psalm 70:4**

**Write about waiting on the Lord and sharing with His gentleness.**

359. You have found your place of refuge in the Lord Jesus Christ. Through His Spirit, you have been comforted. He will always be your refuge when things happen that are difficult and hurt your spirit. Live your life in confidence, knowing that He is with you every day, guiding you and helping you. Be committed in your endeavor to bring others to Christ, who is a refuge to all who desire healing.

> "But let all who take refuge in you be glad; let them ever sing for joy." **Psalm 5:11a**

**Describe how Christ has been your refuge and how gladness fills your heart.**

360. Use the healing that you have received as a springboard for the rest of your life. The Lord has wonderful plans for you. Use the page at the back of this book, entitled, "Impressions from God," as additional space to express the impressions you have received from the Holy Spirit. Rejoice that His love for you is so deep and so profound that He has made plans for you and revealed some of them to you.

> " 'For I know the plans I have for you,' declares the Lord, 'plans to prosper you and not to harm you, plans to give you hope and a future.' " **Jeremiah 29:11**

**Write how you feel that God has made plans for your future.**

________________________________________

________________________________________

________________________________________

________________________________________

________________________________________

________________________________________

________________________________________

________________________________________

________________________________________

________________________________________

________________________________________

361. Always remember this season of tremendous healing with a joyful heart. Think about the spiritual growth God has brought to you through the healing process. You are a different person spiritually than you were. The Lord taught you to depend on the Him through suffering and the healing process. In physical training, resistance builds muscle. In the difficulties of life, the Lord builds strength in you for His ultimate blessing of your life.

> "I will praise you forever for what you have done; in your Name I will hope, for your Name is good. I will praise you in the presence of your saints." **Psalm 52:9**

**Write about praising God for all He has done, for helping you to grow spiritually through the suffering and healing.**

________________________________________________________

________________________________________________________

________________________________________________________

________________________________________________________

________________________________________________________

________________________________________________________

________________________________________________________

________________________________________________________

________________________________________________________

________________________________________________________

________________________________________________________

362. God knows your heart and your commitment to Him. He is ever with you and will help you to continue to grow in His grace. Be strong in the mighty work of God. One way His strength is given to you is through His Word. Make the Word a part of your daily life. Meditate on the truths that are written in it. Sing Scripture. It will bring you even more healing as the years go by.

> "For the eyes of the Lord range throughout the earth to strengthen those whose hearts are fully committed to Him." **2 Chronicles 16:9**

**Write about being strengthened by the Word.**

363. God's work of grace in your life will continue, deepening your relationship with Him. Another part of this work of God's power is the basic discipline of living the Christian life. It is given by the grace of Christ, allowing you to continue to grow in the areas of forgiveness, compassion, and self-control. Christ can help you make the adjustment from a difficult, antagonistic temperament to a calm disposition. He has taken the hurt that once caused you to attack others verbally, and replaced it with a desire to live in peace and the grace to do so. The Holy God is able to do more than you can ask or imagine.

> "Now to Him who is able to do immeasurably more than all we ask or imagine, according to His power that is at work within us, to Him be the glory in the church and in Christ Jesus throughout all generations, for ever and ever! Amen." **Ephesians 3:20,21**

**Write about your new life of discipline in Christ.**

364. Paul has written this powerful prayer not only for the people in the church of Philippi, but for all those who would seek Christ. He prays fervently that you would abound more and more in knowledge and depth of insight. Through the Presence of the Holy Spirit and the power of the Word you will experience this more each day. He will give you insight about people who need a touch of His grace from you or prayer and compassion. He will help you to understand events as they occur. Lean into God for this knowledge and insight.

> "And this is my prayer: that your love may abound more and more in knowledge and depth of insight, so that you may be able to discern what is best and may be pure and blameless until the day of Christ, filled with the fruit of righteousness that comes through Jesus Christ — to the glory and praise of God." **Philippians 1:9–11**

**Write about what really blesses you from this prayer.**

________________________________________

________________________________________

________________________________________

________________________________________

________________________________________

________________________________________

________________________________________

________________________________________

________________________________________

365. The love and tenderness of the Father will continue to cover you. The grace of the Lord Jesus Christ will ease the daily problems of living in this world. The Holy Spirit will keep the flame of your healing burning and continue to fan into flames the gift of your soul. With your whole heart, desire the divine fellowship of the Triune God. Seek God with all that is in you, His righteousness, and sweet love. You will bless many with His love.

> "May the grace of the Lord Jesus Christ, and the love of God, and the fellowship of the Holy Spirit be with you all." **2 Corinthians 13:14**

**Write about pursuing more and more the Triune God.**

## The One, True Healer

This is a book of healing. The focus of the entire process of healing is on the One, True Healer, Jesus Christ. The Word of God points to the healing love of Christ. It is important to understand that every person has sinned and therefore has been separated from God.

> "For all have sinned and fall short of the glory of God."
> **Romans 3:23**

The consequence of all sin is the ultimate death, an eternal separation from God. But God loves you so much that He allowed Jesus to pay the penalty for your sin, that you could be reconciled with God.

> "For the wages of sin is death, but the gift of God is eternal life in Christ Jesus our Lord." **Romans 6:23**

> "For God so loved the world that He gave His one and only Son, that whoever believes in Him shall not perish, but have eternal life." **John 3:16**

Receiving this gift of grace is simple. You can do it now. The moment you do, your healing process will begin. First, confess your own sin, the stuff inside that has blocked you from truly loving yourself, others and God.

> "If we confess our sins, He is faithful and will forgive us our sins and purify us from all unrighteousness."
> **1 John 1:9**

Second, believe and receive the Lord Jesus as your Savior, the One who will cleanse your heart from a life of sin and give you the right to be a child of God.

> "Yet to all who received Him, to those who believed in His Name, He gave the right to become children of God." **John 1:12**

Finally, understand it is by faith in Christ that you are saved and not by anything that you can do or accomplish.

> "For it is by grace you have been saved, through faith—and this is not from yourselves, it is a gift from God—not by works, so that no one can boast." **Ephesians 2:8,9**

If you have not yet personally received Jesus as your Savior, take time now to invite Him into your life. In doing this, you will enter into a personal, saving relationship with God through His Son, Jesus Christ.

**Write how and when this life-changing moment happened for you, so that you may cherish it always.**

## Impressions From God

## Freda Emmons, *Author & Inspirational Speaker*

Freda is passionate about sharing her story, in print and as a speaker. She utilizes humor to infuse the very intense issues of physical and sexual abuse with compassion and tenderness.

Freda is available for small and large group presentations, women's retreats, and venues which support victims in their healing process. For more information, contact Freda at:

Freda Emmons
PO Box 62
Troutdale, Oregon 97060

www.fredaemmons.com
fredaemmons@gmail.com
(503) 539-6326

Made in the USA
Columbia, SC
24 August 2022